SCOTLAND

- A ✓ in the text denotes a highly recommended sight
- A complete A–Z of practical information starts on p.105
- Extensive mapping on cover flaps; Blueprint map on p.105

Printed in Switzerland by Weber SA, Bienne.

1st edition
Reprinted with corrections 1996

Although we make every effort to ensure the accuracy of the information in this guide, changes do occur. If you have any new information, suggestions or corrections to contribute, we would like to hear from you. Please write to Berlitz Publishing at one of the above addresses.

Original text: Don Larrimore
Additional text: Clare Evans Calder
Editors: Romilly Hambling, Corinne Orde
Photography: Darius Koehli
Layout: Suzanna Boyle
Cartography: 🖲 Falk-Verlag, Hamburg

Thanks to: We're grateful to Dick Fotheringham and Meryl A Masterton for their help in the preparation of this book. We would also like to thank the Scottish Tourist Board and, in particular, the information centres at Aberdeen, Alloway, Broadford (Skye), Brodick (Arran), Dumfries, Durness, Edinburgh, Fort William and Oban for their considerable assistance.

Cover photographs: front: *Eilean Donan castle* – Image Bank ©
                      back: *Glenshee* – Berlitz ©

CONTENTS

Scotland and the Scots

Deep green glens which slice through majestic mountains, forbidding castles reflected in dark, peat-stained lochs, moors awash with purple heather or the yellow of broom and gorse, sheep dotting every horizon: Scotland's Highlands, islands and Lowlands are a riot of natural beauty and one of the few remaining wilderness frontiers in all of Europe.

Within easy reach of the cities of Edinburgh, Glasgow, Aberdeen and Dundee are vast tracts of unspoilt country. You might see red deer break cover and golden eagles, or even an osprey, swooping overhead. In coursing streams magnificent salmon and trout challenge the angler, while seals lounge on rocky shores. It's quite possible to walk all day and not see another human being.

Scotland is a land steeped in romantic tradition and stormy history where clan tartans and skirling bagpipes are not mere tourist gimmicks. The cultural mosaic, like the scenery, is hugely varied. Every summer Edinburgh, the intellectually and architecturally stimulating capital, is the scene of a distinguished international festival of music and the arts; and in 1990 Glasgow enjoyed living up to its title of European City of Culture. Elsewhere around the country are staged plays, concerts, Highland gatherings, folk shows and exhibitions of crafts. You can visit some 150 of Scotland's 1,200 castles – some intact, others respectable ruins. There are also unusual museums, baronial mansions, ancient abbeys, formal gardens and archaeological sites that invite exploration. Glasgow is the home of one of Europe's great art galleries.

Happily, what people say about Scotland's weather isn't always true. Between May and October there are invariably hours and even whole days of hot sunshine, interrupting the rain, mist and bracing winds which perhaps keep the Scots so hardy. Interestingly enough, Scotland in an average year **5** enjoys as much sun as London. Sightseers and photographers appreciate the amazing visibility to be had on clear days. The cold, snowy winters present no problem to skiers, though they are less fun in remote villages isolated by heavy snows.

Covering the northernmost third of the United Kingdom,

Entertainment in Scotland is never hard to find, especially on city streets in the summer.

Scotland (as some natives like to put it) crowns Great Britain. The country's 30,000 square miles (77,000sq km – about the same size as South Carolina) are home to some 5 million Scots, making one-tenth of the total population of the United Kingdom. Mountain barriers no longer divide the country as they did in the heyday of the Highland clans, but formidable peaks certainly do dominate the landscape. Ben Nevis, whose summit rises to 4,406ft (1,343m), is the highest mountain in Britain.

The wildly irregular coastline, incessantly pounded by the Atlantic and the North Sea, has both forbidding cliffs and sweeping sandy beaches. The sea flows in to fill many of the country's 300 lochs (Scots never call them 'lakes'). Along the west coast some visitors are surprised to find flourishing subtropical gardens – a bonus of the warming Gulf Stream close offshore.

Scotland's territorial area includes 790 islands: most are visited only by sea birds, but 130 are inhabited, and a few are popular tourist destinations which can easily be reached by ferry or plane.

Constitutionally linked to England for nearly three centuries, in many respects Scotland is still a land that keeps proudly unto itself. It prints its own stamps and currency (British versions circulate as well), maintains independent educational and judicial systems, its own church, as well as a native tongue, Gaelic, still spoken in the Western Highlands and Islands.

Since 1975 the country has been divided into nine regions and three island areas. Within the regions are 53 districts, a confusing administrative re-ordering that dissolved such familiar counties as Perthshire and Aberdeenshire. To sort out any muddle, efficient tourist information centres operate all over the country.

Everywhere you'll make the acquaintance of Scots who are enormously friendly and helpful to strangers. Smiles are genuine, humour is jovially sharp and there always seems to be time to chat. Even in tiny villages you may be struck by the eloquence of the people. This may reflect the emphasis placed on education. (In the 17th century Scotland had four

Ullapool, in the north west, is an important fishing centre and a ferry terminal for the islands.

universities while England still had only two.) Indeed, you'll find that most Scots have an independent view to air on just about every issue, especially political ones.

Prepare for a pleasant surprise if you expect all Scots to live up to their reputation for meanness. A few tight-fisted individuals may linger here and there, but generosity to friends and strangers is something you'll experience almost everywhere in Scotland.

The Scots do live up to their reputation for enjoying a drink or two. The consequential high level of alcoholism and all it may bring in its wake are an acknowledged problem. Heart disease is another worry in Scotland, with the national diet – low on fresh fruit and vegetables but high in fat – being held largely responsible.

True grit! Traditional Highland Games during summer are a real test of strength for many Scots.

One subject that's certain to fire the hearts of most Scotsmen is soccer, with the rivalry between two Glasgow teams, Rangers and Celtic, inspiring the most passionate debate. The national team also arouses fierce loyalties, although fans contain their ardour and have the reputation of being some of the best-behaved in Europe.

Over the centuries the Scots have made their mark on all corners of the globe: they were frontiersmen in north America, explorers in Africa, pioneers in Australia. For various reasons, most of them economic, they have often settled down far afield. Nowadays about ten times more people of Scottish birth or ancestry live abroad than those at home. Intellectually, the contribution made by Scots to world science, medicine and industry has been little short of astonishing.

Above all, what binds the Scots together is a love of the country plus a strong sense of community and national identity. Together these feelings inspire the by and large friendly rivalry that the Scots feel towards their neighbours south of the border.

Cobbles and crow-stepped gables help bring history to life down Edinburgh's Royal Mile.

All over Scotland you will see and hear the exhortation to 'Haste ye back' ('Come back soon'). After sampling the extraordinary beauty and diversity of this delightful country, you'll most certainly want to. **9**

A Brief History

It all began over 8,000 years ago – and it's never been easy. The earliest settlers, drifting north from England or across from the area of present-day Ulster, fished and hunted along the west coast of Scotland.

By about 4000 BC more sophisticated immigrants from western Europe, Britain and Ireland had begun farming and raising stock in Scotland, using pottery and burying their dead in stone tombs. Recently, west of Aberdeen, archaeologists discovered the remains of a huge timbered building from this era, predating Stonehenge by 1,000 years. Now known as Balbridie Hall, it is the oldest wooden structure ever found in the British Isles.

Scotland's famous megalithic monuments – the Standing Stones of Callanish on Lewis in the Outer Hebrides, and the Ring of Brodgar and Standing Stones of Stenness on Mainland in the Orkney Islands – were erected between 2000 and 1500 BC by a race that appears to have had its origins in the Mediterranean.

During the Bronze and Iron ages Scotland was settled by various tribes that spoke forms of Celtic (which survives in Britain as Gaelic and Welsh). Inhabitants south of the Forth-Clyde isthmus were Britons, while those living to the north became known as Picts. These primitive tribes were no match for the Roman legions which marched north under Agricola and defeated the Picts in AD 84 at the battle of Mons Graupius in north-east Scotland.

As a line of defence against the tiresome Picts, the Romans built a series of forts all across Scotland from Meigle (north west of Dundee) to the River Clyde, south of Loch Lomond. It was the northernmost limit of their vast empire. They later withdrew to the line marked by Hadrian's Wall, which is close to the present Scottish-English border.

Towards the end of the 2nd century Pictish warriors raided south across both lines, provoking a retaliatory assault by Septimus Severus in 208. This

HISTORICAL LANDMARKS

2nd c. AD   Romans retreat from northern strongholds and build Hadrian's Wall.

5th-6th c.   Gaelic-speaking Scots arrive from Ireland.

563   St Columba reaches Iona.

1018   Scotland's southern boundary established.

1069   Malcolm III (Canmore) marries the English Margaret.

1296   Edward I sacks Berwick and steals the Stone of Destiny from Scone.

1297   Battle of Stirling Bridge; Scots defeat the English.

1306   Robert the Bruce crowned King of Scotland.

1314   Battle of Bannockburn (June 24). Robert the Bruce defeats the English under Edward II.

1328   Treaty of Northampton recognizes independence of Scotland.

1513   Battle of Flodden; around 10,000 Scots killed by the English.

1542   Mary, Queen of Scots, born at Linlithgow Palace.

1567   Mary forced to abdicate and imprisoned on Loch Leven. She escapes in 1568 but spends the rest of her life imprisoned in England.

1603   Union of Crowns.

17th c.   Internal religious fighting, the Covenanters against the English forces of Cromwell.

1692   Massacre of Glencoe (February 13).

1707   Act of Union; Scotland and England become one kingdom.

18th c.   Jacobite risings in 1715 and 1745 under Bonnie Prince Charlie and the Old Pretender. 'Scottish Enlightenment' in the south of the country (Edinburgh), with Robert Burns and Sir Walter Scott, amongst others.

1780   Highland Clearances begin.

19th c.   Scotland's profile is raised due to the patronage of Queen Victoria.

20th c.   Resurgence of nationalist spirit and growing discontent with Westminster government.

was the last important Roman incursion into Scotland.

The Scots entered the scene during the 5th to 6th centuries. A Gaelic-speaking tribe from Ireland, they founded a shaky kingdom in Argyll known as Dalriada that was constantly menaced by the Picts. Then, in AD 563, St Columba came from Ireland to bolster the morale of his fellow Celtic Christians. For over 30 years, from the remote western island of Iona, he spread the faith that would eventually provide the basis for the unification of Scotland. Tiny Iona, with its abbey and royal graveyard, remains one of the most venerated sites in Christendom (see pp.82-83).

The Norse Invasion

Scotland was among the areas that were repeatedly savaged from the late 8th century as the Vikings swarmed over Europe. Permanent Norse strongholds were set up in the Orkneys and Hebrides and on the northern mainland. The Scandinavian

warriors greatly weakened the Picts in 839, enabling a Gaelic chief, Kenneth MacAlpin, to become king of both the Scots and the Picts.

In 1018 this kingdom, led by Malcolm II, defeated the Northumbrians from the south at the battle of Carham and extended its domain to the present southern boundary of Scotland. The 'murder most foul' of Malcolm's grandson, Duncan II, by Macbeth was the inspiration for the great Shakespearean tragedy.

Malcolm III, also known as Malcolm Canmore, changed the course of Scottish history through his marriage in 1069 to an English princess. This was the determinedly pious Queen Margaret, who later became a saint (see p.26). She and her sons brought a powerful English influence and atmosphere to both the Celtic church and the monarchy as

*M*elrose Abbey is one of four in the Borders built by David I but destroyed by the Reformation.

Scotland continued its development into a feudal kingdom.

Margaret's sixth son, David I (1124-53), is remembered for founding such great abbeys as Melrose and Jedburgh in the Borders (see pp.37-38). King David also fostered the start of the peaceful penetration into Scotland of Norman influence. This did not mean a wholesale 'Norman Conquest' such as took place in England, but the spread of French, the building of many castles and churches and, eventually, the absorption of another culture into the Scottish mainstream.

The Shaping of Scotland

Progress, prosperity and the stirrings of national consciousness marked the long reign of King Alexander III (1249-86). At the battle of Largs in 1263 Alexander's forces trounced King Haakon of Norway, compelling the Norsemen to leave the western islands for good. Under a peace treaty the Norse were allowed to retain only the Orkneys and Shetlands, which **13** came under Scottish rule some 200 years later.

The death of Alexander in a riding accident touched off a succession crisis and a long, bloody struggle for Scottish independence. In the midst of the civil strife provoked by no fewer than 13 rival claimants to the throne, King Edward I of England was invited to arbitrate. Seizing the opportunity, he chose John Balliol to be his vassal king of Scots. However, in 1295 Balliol allied himself with France (then at war with England) and renounced his fealty to Edward. In retaliation the English king sacked the burgh of Berwick, crushed the Scots at Dunbar, swept north, seizing the great castles, and carried off from Scone Palace the Sacred Stone of Destiny on which all Scottish monarchs had been crowned. (The stone is still in Westminster Abbey in London.)

Chafing at military occupation, the Scots, led by William Wallace, revolted once more in 1297 and defeated the English at Stirling Bridge. A year later Edward responded by routing Wallace at Falkirk, the English bowmen killing some 15,000 Scots. (In 1305 the outlawed Wallace was captured, taken to London and brutally executed; Edward had parts of his body displayed around Scotland.)

Robert the Bruce looks down to the field at Bannockburn where he quashed the English in 1314.

Then came Robert Bruce, another revered champion of the Scots – even though he sacrilegiously killed his rival in a church before having himself crowned king at Scone Palace in 1306. Forced to flee to Ireland, Bruce returned the next year to subdue his Scottish opponents. Edward died before he could deal with this new upstart, and his weak son, Edward II, was thoroughly defeated by Bruce's forces at the watershed battle of Bannockburn in 1314. Bruce continued to hammer away at the English until 1328, when Edward III signed a treaty that recognized the independence of Scotland. Robert Bruce died the following year, honoured as medieval Scotland's saviour.

The Stewarts

It was not a healthy time to be a Scottish king. The Stewart monarchs James I, II and III, who reigned successively between 1406 and 1488, came to power while still children and all died violently. James I was kidnapped and held captive for 18 years; after a brief reign he was murdered. James II was killed by an exploding gun; and James III was assassinated before he was 40.

During this period Scotland extended its territorial boundaries to their present limits by capturing the Orkney and Shetland islands from Norway in 1472. Today, many place names still recall the centuries of Norse occupation.

James IV, who ruled from 1488 to 1513, strengthened the monarchy considerably. In the western Highlands and islands he succeeded in putting down the rebellious Macdonald clan chiefs, who had been styling themselves 'Lords of the Isles' since the mid-14th century. Against the English he didn't do nearly so well: in 1513, to honour the 'auld alliance' with France, James led his Scottish troops in an invasion that penetrated only a few miles over the border to Flodden. In the ensuing, bitterly remembered battle the Scots were crushed by the English under the Earl of Surrey. In all about 10,000 lost their lives, including the **15**

*M*ary, Queen of Scots, slept at this house in Jedburgh while visiting in 1556.

king himself and most of the peerage. The defeat at Flodden was the worst military disaster Scotland ever suffered.

One result of the battle was to bring the infant James V to the throne. When he came of age he had his own sister burnt **16** as a witch, conducted bloody struggles against the Scottish clans, resisted the expansion of Henry VIII's Reformation, promoted local Scottish justice and married first one French woman, then a second called Mary of Guise. James died prematurely in 1542, six days after his wife had given birth to a daughter, his only heir.

Mary Queen of Scots

The adventurous life, loves and death of this queen have captivated the imagination of generations of Scots. Henry VIII attempted to force a treaty that betrothed her to his son. Infuriated when this failed, he sent his troops on the rampage through southern Scotland. At the age of five Mary was sent to France for safekeeping; in time, her pro-Catholic mother, supported by French forces, took over as regent. This led to an increasing sense of anger felt by many Scots.

Little more than a child herself, Mary was married to the boy-heir to the French throne. He died soon after becoming king, however, and in 1561

Mary, a devout young Catholic widow, returned to Scotland to assume her throne. There she found the Protestant Reformation in full cry, led by the fiery John Knox. Roman Catholicism had been abolished and the French troops had been sent home.

Most of her seven years as resident Queen of Scots Mary spent at Holyroodhouse Palace in Edinburgh. She insisted on being allowed to practise her Catholic faith but placed no bar on religious freedom in her realm. In 1565 Mary married Henry, Lord Darnley, a controversial young nobleman. The next year she bore a son, the future James VI. Darnley was implicated in the murder of Mary's confidential secretary at Holyroodhouse (see p.31) and was killed in 1567. Many suspected Mary of conniving in the murder of her husband and doubts crystallized when, a few months later, she married one of the ringleaders of the plot, the newly divorced Protestant Earl of Bothwell.

That was too much for some of her subjects, who demanded her death by burning. Mary tried to flee but was captured, imprisoned in an island castle on Loch Leven and forced to abdicate in July 1567 in favour of her infant son. Seeking refuge in England where, at least to Catholics, she seemed to have a legitimate claim to the throne held by her cousin Elizabeth, Mary was instead kept in captivity for nearly 20 years until, in 1587, she was finally beheaded.

Toward Union with England

In the wake of Mary's removal from the scene, Protestantism became the official religion of Scotland. After an interval of rule by regents (1567-78) James VI assumed the throne as the country's first Protestant king. When Elizabeth died in 1603, James, as the heir, rode south to claim the English throne as James I. For most of his reign he ruled his native land from afar, as did his Stuart successors. Unfortunately, the Union of Crowns did not bring instant harmony to relations **17**

between the two traditionally antagonistic neighbours.

The 17th century witnessed fierce religious and political struggles in Scotland. James' son Charles I (1625-49) had to face opposition from Scottish churchmen – and even rioting – provoked by his attempts to impose an English version of the prayer book. In 1638 Scots around the country signed the National Covenant, which insisted on the right to their own form of Presbyterian worship.

In the civil war that broke out in England, the Covenanters at first backed Parliament against Charles, who was beheaded in 1649. After this they threw in their lot with Charles II, which led to defeat at Dunbar by Cromwell. Scotland endured nine years of dictatorship under his Commonwealth.

Scotland's bloody religious fighting continued for a long time after the restoration of the monarchy in 1660. Extreme Covenanters in the Highlands

*D*ramatic Glen Coe was the scene of one of the bloodiest massacres in Scottish history.

were severely persecuted during the so-called 'killing time'. However, when James VII was dethroned in the revolution of 1688, Presbyterianism was formally established as the state religion of Scotland.

Highland clans were forced to take an oath of loyalty to the new king of England, William of Orange (1689-1702). When the small Macdonald clan of Glen Coe was slow to deliver its pledge, a force of soldiers led by Campbell of Glenlyon slaughtered 38 of its members. Women and children were not spared. This Massacre of Glen Coe on 13 February 1692, one of the blacker episodes in Scottish history, immeasurably deepened any clan hatreds and Highland resentment of the monarchy.

In 1707, despite widespread Scottish opposition, England and Scotland signed the Act of Union, which made them one kingdom, Great Britain, with the same parliament and flag. The Scots would have minority representation in the upper and lower houses at Westminster that reflected their population and wealth. They were allowed to keep their own courts and very different legal system, and the status of the national Presbyterian church was guaranteed. Today it seems that the union of the two countries was historically inevitable. Scottish nationalism, however, was not so easily subdued.

The Risings

Four times in the next 40 years the Jacobites (Stuart loyalists) tried to restore the exiled royal family to the throne, which was now occupied by a family of German (Hanoverian) origin. In 1708 the son of James VII, known as the 'Old Pretender', arrived with a French invasion force in the Firth of Forth but was prevented from landing.

In 1715 the Jacobites were slightly more successful under the Earl of Mar who, as the **19**

*T*he monument at Culloden honours the 1,200 Jacobite soldiers killed in 1746 at the Battle of Culloden Moor.

leader of some 12,000 men, managed briefly to hold Perth, Inverness and the north-east coast. They hoped for French help, though this never came. The Pretender arrived months too late to rally any further support from an apathetic or pro-government public, and, after the inconclusive battle of Sheriffmuir (near Dunblane),

the rebellion remembered as the 'Fifteen' fell into disarray. A Highland rising in 1719 had the support of a small Spanish fleet, but quickly failed.

The most serious Jacobite effort was the Rising of 1745, which furnished the material for much heroic – and tragic – Scottish legend. It was headed by the Young Pretender, Prince

Charles Edward Stuart. Ever since known by the nickname Bonnie Prince Charlie, this grandson of James VII was 24 years old when he sailed from France disguised as a divinity student to land in Scotland in July 1745, bent on recovering the throne for the house of Stuart. Within as little as two months he had rallied enough clan warriors to sweep through Scotland, occupying Perth and Edinburgh and defeating a government army at Preston-pans. In early November he invaded England, pushing as far south as Derby, 130 miles (210km) north of London, by 4 December.

However, English Jacobites failed to come to the aid of the rebellion and Charles' troops were hopelessly outnumbered. Reluctantly he agreed with the advice of his brilliant tactician, Lord George Murray, to retreat north and, by 20 December, they were back in Scotland. Despite an impressive victory over the English at Falkirk in January, from this time on it was downhill for Charles and the Jacobite cause.

At the battle of Culloden Moor, which was fought near Inverness on 16 April 1746, the weary Highlanders were subjected to a crushing defeat at the hands of superior government forces under the Duke of Cumberland. In less than an hour about 1,200 of Charles' men were killed; many others, wounded and captured, were treated in a brutal manner that earned Cumberland the lasting soubriquet of 'Butcher'. The '45 was over, but feelings run deep even today.

Charles escaped, spending five months as a fugitive in the Highlands and western islands before leaving his country for good aboard a French ship.

The Aftermath

Although the Jacobite cause was finished, Highlanders had to face the harsh consequences of joining the rebellion. The British government moved to pacify the region, confiscating arms and setting up garrisons, disabling the clan structure, suppressing Gaelic and even, for several decades, banning **21**

Great Scots

JOHN LOGIE BAIRD (1888-1946): scientist credited with invention of television – the first to transmit TV signals over a distance.

JAMES BOSWELL (1740-95): biographer of Samuel Johnson.

ROBERT BURNS (1759-96): Scotland's leading poet and song writer, wrote *Tam o'Shanter* and *Auld Lang Syne*.

THOMAS CARLYLE (1795-1881): historian, rewrote classic *French Revolution* after first draft was accidentally burnt.

ALEXANDER FLEMING (1881-1955): bacteriologist, discoverer of penicillin.

DAVID HUME (1711-76): philosopher, historian, author of *An Enquiry Concerning Human Nature*.

LORD WILLIAM THOMPSON KELVIN (1824-1907): scientist, pioneer of trans-Atlantic telegraphy, developed theory of tides.

JOHN KNOX (1505-72): led Scotland's Protestant Reformation.

DAVID LIVINGSTONE (1813-73): missionary explorer, mapped Zambesi River, lakes and much of African interior.

JOHN L MCADAM (1756-1836): engineer whose waterproof road surface bears his name.

SIR WALTER SCOTT (1771-1832): romantic poet (*The Lady of the Lake*), novelist (*Waverley, Rob Roy*), Scottish patriot.

SIR JAMES SIMPSON (1811-70): medical scientist, pioneered use of chloroform as anaesthetic in surgery.

ADAM SMITH (1723-90): scholar, founded science of political economy, wrote *The Wealth of Nations*.

ROBERT LOUIS STEVENSON (1850-94): novelist and poet, wrote *Treasure Island, The Strange Case of Dr Jekyll and Mr Hyde*.

JAMES WATT (1736-1819): inventor of modern condensing steam engine.

the wearing of the kilt. For almost a century after the year 1780, the families of thousands of crofters (farmers of smallholdings) were compelled to abandon their homes to make room for wealthier sheep farmers from the south under the infamous policy that became known as the Highland Clearances. Some were evicted, and many emigrated in poverty to the United States, Canada and Australia. When Britain went to war with Napoleonic France, nearly 40,000 men were raised for new Highland regiments. They acquitted themselves with distinction.

In the less troubled southern part of Scotland the capital, Edinburgh, began its development into an intellectual and cultural centre of international standing, which it remains to this day. The work of Scottish scientists, philosophers, writers, explorers, engineers and industrialists became famous all over the world. Individual Scots went south and made notable contributions to the life of the United Kingdom, which they had made their home.

A symbolic turning point came in 1822 when George IV made the first state visit to Scotland by a British monarch in well over a century. Tartans and clan regalia were paraded at Holyroodhouse Palace and the king himself donned a kilt in festivities organized by Sir Walter Scott.

Later, Queen Victoria 'discovered' Scotland and bought Balmoral Castle, which is still regularly used as a summer home by the royal family.

Recent years have seen a resurgence of Scottish national spirit – largely the result of frustration at the decline of the British economy, a feeling that the country has not received its fair share of the revenue from oil discovered off its shores, and hostility to a succession of Conservative governments in a traditional Labour area. Even so, the Scottish National Party continues to win only a small number of seats in Parliament and, for the time being at least, Scotland's fortunes, political and economic, are inextricably interlinked with those of its 'auld enemy', England. **23**

Where to Go

Scotland, 275 miles (442km) from north to south (not counting all the islands) and as wide as 150 miles (241km), is far too large and full of sights to 'do' on a touring holiday unless it lasts for months. With or without a car, it is best to concentrate on one or two areas. There is a very useful public transport system (see p.127), air services connecting various points on the mainland and the islands, plus several guided excursions by bus and boat from most tourist centres.

Getting from place to place is by and large fairly straightforward, as Scotland now has a good network of roads. However, if you are travelling around the West Highlands, you should allow plenty of time for your journey as many of the roads have only a single lane with frequent scooped out 'passing places', where you or the oncoming vehicle must pull over to the side to let the other pass by. This can make progress very slow.

In this section sightseeing highlights are described in the areas of Scotland which are most visited by tourists. Local details may be obtained from an extensive network of tourist information offices.

Edinburgh

The proud capital of Scotland proves a pleasant surprise for most visitors on account of its elegance and civilization – particularly when the sun is shining. Both the Old Town up against the rock of Edinburgh Castle and the New Town across the way are well worth exploring. You will find some of the most impressive buildings in Europe and a markedly congenial atmosphere – an unexpected bonus in a city of nearly half a million people.

Edinburgh's seven hills look northwards over the great Firth of Forth estuary or southwards to gentle green countryside that rises into hills. Everywhere you climb there's a fine panorama; from on high you might well see one of the city's

24 golf courses – after all, it *is* the most Scottish of games. Tour guides boast that Edinburgh is probably 1,500 years old and has been the capital of Scotland since 1437. They point out homes of famous people you never knew came from here. Despite all these echoes of the past, the city today seems decidedly young and vibrant; it is at its liveliest – and most crowded – during the three-week Edinburgh Festival which takes place each August–September.

Many of the city's principal sights are within easy walking distance of each other; most

The skyline of the Royal Mile – historic buildings enjoy fabulous views over the city and gardens.

can be reached by public bus, and throughout the day excursion coaches depart from Waverley Bridge, near the local tourist information office.

EDINBURGH CASTLE

Heavy with history, Scotland's most popular tourist attraction stands on an extinct volcano, high above the city. It is not **25**

*E*dinburgh's buskers enjoy the summer; plenty of puff and a set of bagpipes make good earners.

known how long ago Edinburgh's history began on this great rock, but a stone fortification was definitely erected late in the 7th century and the first proper castle was built in the 11th century.

Two guards from the Scottish regiments are posted at the first gate leading up the cobblestone rampways to the castle. The impressive black naval cannons poking through the ramparts have never been fired, but you'll see the cannon which booms out over the city every weekday to mark 1pm. Why isn't it fired at noon? 'Remember where you are,' quips the guide, 'One cannon shot at one o'clock is much cheaper than 12 at noon'.

Tiny **St Margaret's Chapel** with its plain white interior is the oldest building in Edinburgh and the oldest church in use in Scotland. It was built by Queen Margaret in about 1076 and has survived assaults over the centuries that destroyed the other structures on Castle Rock. The Norman chapel has been simply restored and is kept decorated with flowers by Scotswomen named Margaret.

Close by is an oddity – the world's most spectacular canine graveyard. In a niche that overlooks the city you'll find the **Cemetery for Soldiers' Dogs** with the tombs of regimental mascots. Further along is the Lyon's Den where James

VI kept his pet lion (not open to the public).

In the Palace Yard is the **Great Hall**, which claims the finest hammer-beam ceiling in Britain. Built in 1502, the oak timbers are joined together without a single nail, screw or bolt. It is here that Scotland's parliament met for a century. Among the arms on display is a hefty claymore (from the Gaelic word for broadsword), whilst the military museum exhibits a vast array of regimental paraphernalia.

Queen Mary's Rooms in the royal apartments include a very small chamber where she gave birth to James VI (later James I of England).

The castle's greatest treasure, the crown, sceptre and sword of Scotland, are displayed in the **Crown Room**. At times, more than 10,000

The castle and Princes Street Gardens – where better to while away an afternoon?

also some dazzling jewellery on display.

Note: The entrance to Edinburgh Castle lies just beyond the **Esplanade**, which was at one time a site for the execution of witches, later became a parade ground, and is now a parking lot where the famous Military Tattoo is performed during the annual Edinburgh International Festival.

In the back vault of the **French prisons** you will find **Mons Meg**, a stout cannon that was forged in Mons – hence the name – in the 15th century. The five-ton monster ingloriously blew up 200 years later while firing a salute to the Duke of York.

For no extra charge you can join the group of one of the witty and lore-loving palace guides. Edinburgh Castle is open to the public every day from 9.30am until 6pm.

viewers a day file through here to see the oldest royal regalia in Europe. The gold and pearl crown was first used for the coronation of Robert Bruce in 1306, although it was altered in 1540, and Charles II wore it for the last time in 1651. The sword and sceptre were given to James IV by Popes Alexander VI and Julius II. There is

28

THE ROYAL MILE

The Royal Mile, along the ridge from Edinburgh Castle to the royal palace, Holyroodhouse, is all downhill. The Old Town's famous thoroughfare, its cobbles now smoothed, is actually about 1¼ miles (2km) long – the Scottish mile was longer than the English.

Edinburghers of this area of high tenements and narrow closes (entryways) seem to take delight in recounting how the residents used to toss slops and refuse from windows after a perfunctory shout of 'Gardy-loo!' – the equivalent of *'gare de l'eau'*. That meant centuries of rampant disease and a decidedly unpleasant reputation for a city so graced with intellectual genius.

Today, odourless, tidy and lined with historic buildings, the Royal Mile assumes five names as it descends: Castlehill, Lawnmarket, High Street, Canongate and Abbey Strand.

On Castlehill the **Camera Obscura** at the top of the Outlook Tower offers a fascinating 15-minute show – make sure

to go when the weather is dry – plus exhibitions on related topics. After climbing the 98 steps to a darkened chamber, you can enjoy living panoramas of the city projected on to a circular table-screen to the accompaniment of a wonderful commentary.

Opposite, in the **Scotch Whisky Heritage Centre**, you will be transported (in a barrel!) through the history of Scotland's 'water of life'.

Further along, in James Court, Samuel Johnson once visited his biographer, James Boswell, whilst in Brodie's Close the popular local story of Deacon Brodie is recalled: a respected city official and **29** carpenter by day, he was a burglar by night (having taken wax impressions of his clients' house keys). Finally arrested and condemned to death, he tried to escape death by wearing a steel collar under his shirt. Unfortunately for him, the gallows, which he himself had designed, worked perfectly. His double life was to inspire R L Stevenson to write *Dr Jekyll and Mr Hyde*.

A brief detour down George IV Bridge takes you to the statuette of **Greyfriars Bobby**. This Skye terrier waited by his master's grave in nearby Greyfriars Churchyard for 14 years until dying of old age in 1872. Admiring the dog's fidelity, authorities made Bobby a freeman of the city – meaning he had the vote before women, they'll tell you.

Across the road in Chambers Street stands the **Royal Museum of Scotland** with a whole range of interesting collections and exhibitions and plenty for children to enjoy on a wet day.

Back along the Royal Mile, **St Giles Cathedral**, the High Kirk of Scotland, dominates Parliament Square. Its famous tower spire was built in 1495 as a replica of the Scottish crown. The oldest elements of St Giles are the huge 12th-century pillars that support the

The Palace of Holyroodhouse dates from around 1500 and lies at the east end of the Royal Mile.

spire, but there was probably a church on the site since 854. John Knox preached here and is thought to be buried in the rear graveyard. The spectacular, soaring Norman interior of St Giles, with splendid stained glass, is filled with memorials recalling the great moments of Scottish history.

Most beautiful is the fairly recent (1911) **Thistle Chapel**, ornately carved out of Scottish oak. You'll see a stall for the queen and a princely seat for each of the 16 Knights of the Thistle, Scotland's oldest order of chivalry.

The **Museum of Childhood** – a favourite with children and adults alike – is further down the Royal Mile, as is **Huntly House** and the **People's Story**, a history of Edinburgh life seen through the eyes of its inhabitants.

The celebrated royal palace of **Holyroodhouse** began life in about 1500 as a mere guest house for the adjacent, now-ruined, abbey. Much expanded and rebuilt in the 17th century, visiting monarchs have often resided here. During the summer months, Holyroodhouse is closed to the public for the week or so that the royal family is in residence.

In the long Picture Gallery, guides shepherd groups of visitors past 111 portraits purportedly of Scottish kings and which were dashed off between 1684 and 1686 by Jacob de Wet, a Dutchman armed with much imagination, brushes and paint.

In King James' Tower, connected by an inner stairway, are the apartments of Darnley and Mary Queen of Scots. A plaque marks the spot where the unfortunate Rizzio, Mary's secretary, was stabbed over 56 times with a dagger.

THE NEW TOWN

Until late in the 18th century all of Edinburgh was confined to the crowded, unhealthy Old Town along the ridge from the Castle. The population, which numbered about 25,000 in 1700, had nearly tripled by 1767, when James Craig won a planning competition for an extension to the city. **31**

The lawns around Scott Monument offer a break from bustling adjacent Princes Street.

With significant help from the noted Robert Adam, the resulting New Town has become the most complete complex of Georgian architecture.

At the centre of it is Edinburgh's main thoroughfare, the bustling Princes Street. At the far end is Waverley Market Shopping Centre, a mall of shops and restaurants on two levels, with the railway station below and tourist information office above.

A foetid stretch of water called Nor' Loch was drained and made into **Princes Street Gardens**, the city's attractive green centrepiece. Rising from the gardens is the landmark spire of the **Scott Monument**, which has a statue of Sir Walter with his dog, statuettes of Scott's literary characters and 287 steps to the top. On climbing them you get a certificate as well as an excellent panorama. A **floral clock** with some 24,000 plants is also found in Princes Street Gardens.

A sloping road, known as the Mound, passes through the gardens. Here, behind the Royal Scottish Academy, you will find the **National Gallery of Scotland**, a small but distinguished collection featuring the great painters. Look out for Van Dyck's *Lomellini Family*, Rubens' gory *The Feast of Herod*, Velásquez' *Old Woman Cooking Eggs,* and four Rembrandt portraits. The English school is represented by Reynolds, Turner and Gainsborough, and you will see many paintings by the city's own artist Henry Raeburn. The gallery also has a selection of Impressionist works and a collection of Scottish paintings.

Charlotte Square, the neoclassical centrepiece of the New Town, spreads north of Princes Street. The 11 houses which form the north side of the square and have symmetrical façades are considered to be the finest work by Robert Adam, Scotland's most celebrated 18th-century architect.

No 7 Charlotte Square has been converted into an authentic Georgian show-house by the National Trust for Scotland. In the dining room you will see a covetable table setting of Wedgwood and Sheffield, and in the bed-chamber there is a marvellous medicine chest and a 19th-century water closet called 'the receiver'. The house is open from Easter until October.

The excellent **Scottish National Gallery of Modern Art** is on Belford Road, and is well worth a visit. Displaying only part of its large collection, the gallery also puts on fine touring exhibitions.

Along Inverleith Row extend the 75 acres (30ha) of the much-admired **Royal Botanic Gardens** with probably the world's largest collection of rhododendrons and a remarkable rock garden, as well as cavernous plant houses.

A colony of some 200 penguins is the main attraction at Edinburgh's **zoo**, set in rolling parkland in the western suburb of Corstorphine. Be sure you take your camera.

The South East

From Edinburgh there are several excursions you can take by bus to points of interest in the countryside. One of the closest is the huge **Hopetoun House**, an Adam mansion near South Queensbury (10 miles/16km west of Edinburgh). The house offers fine original furnishings as well as paintings by Dutch and Italian masters and, throughout its 100 acres (41ha) of grounds, four-horned St Kilda sheep and red deer.

Nearby at **Linlithgow**, overlooking the loch, stand the extensive ruins of the fortified palace which was the birthplace of Mary Queen of Scots in 1542. Alongside is one of the best medieval churches in Britain, **St Michael's**, where a well-documented ghost is said to have warned James IV not to fight against England – shortly before he and so many Scots were killed at Flodden.

Golf courses, sandy duned beaches and pleasant villages make **East Lothian** a popular holiday district. At **Dirleton** original stone cottages set off a large village green beneath a ruined castle. In good weather you can take a boat excursion from North Berwick around the towering **Bass Rock** where some 8,000 gannets far outnumber the puffins, kittiwakes, shags and cormorants.

Ashore, the formidable reddish ruins of the 600-year-old **Tantallon Castle** are seen up high on a seaside cliff. Queen Victoria visited this fortress of the Black Douglas clan in 1898, and presumably peered (as you also can) into the well cut 90ft (27m) through sheer rock. To the east at beautiful **Seacliff Bay** you walk along a rocky shore to what is said to be Britain's smallest harbour.

Inland the now sleepy hamlet of **Whitekirk** still has its large church, but no longer the reputed Holy Well which during the 15th century attracted thousands of pilgrims, includ-

Forget about the sands of time and relax on the beaches of the East Coast, south of Edinburgh.

ing Pope Pius II. At East Linton you might stop to inspect **Preston Mill**, restored as it was 350 years ago. It claims to be the oldest water mill in the country that is capable of producing meal.

A walk round the little town of **Haddington** reveals a well-preserved 18th-century atmosphere. Many of its 100 buildings are cited for their historic or architectural interest.

Rolling green wooded farmland runs on from Lothian into Scotland's south Borders region, notably along the River Tweed, which is best known for giving its name to a twilled fabric. The hilly countryside around **Peebles**, a nice riverside resort, is worth exploring, and particularly the beautiful Manor Valley.

To the east along the River Tweed, near Innerleithen, is **Traquair House**, which dates back some 1,000 years. In all, 27 Scottish and English kings have stayed at Traquair, which is full of such curiosities as a secret stairway from a priest's

Sir Walter Scott's collection of arms is on show at Abbotsford, his fine home on the River Tweed.

room and a 14th-century hand-printed bible.

Abbotsford, further down the Tweed past Galashiels, is the somewhat elaborate house where Sir Walter Scott spent the last 20 years of his life. Visitors may inspect his armouries as well as rooms containing unusual items which Scott collected. The house is open daily except in winter.

THE BORDER ABBEYS

All founded in the 12th century during the reign of David I, Scotland's four great southern monasteries stand in varying degrees of ruin today. All are worth a visit. Always vulnerable to invading forces from England, the abbeys endured frequent sacking before being restored, then destroyed again.

At **Melrose Abbey**, which is strikingly set off by close-trimmed lawns, you can still see part of the original, high-arching stone church. There is a small museum which is crowded with relics and a lovely formal garden opposite the entrance.

Dryburgh is probably the most beautiful of the four abbeys, and sits among stately beeches and cedars. Some of the monks' cloister survives, but little now remains of the church. Here are the graves of Sir Walter Scott and Field Marshal Earl Haig from World War I. At Bemersyde Hill, which is reached from Dryburgh via Gattonside by a beautiful tree-tunnelled road, you can enjoy **Scott's View**, which used to be the writer's favourite scenic spot.

Only one arcaded transept tower and a façade remain in the market town of **Kelso** to suggest the original dimensions of its abbey, the oldest and once the richest southern Scottish monastery.

Closer to the English border on the River Tweed, **Jedburgh Abbey** is a far more complete structure. The main aisle of the **37**

A macabre memento of past monarchs at Jedburgh – the death mask of Mary Queen of Scots.

Central Scotland

With its proud Renaissance castle commanding the major route between the Lowlands and the Highlands, **Stirling** for centuries saw much of Scotland's worst warfare. Guides at the **castle** regale visitors with tales of sieges, intrigue, dastardly murders and atrocities, and an audio-visual presentation just off the castle esplanade brings the savage saga vividly to life. If you wish to take a break, walk along the ramparts and gaze over the now placid plains from this lofty fortress rock.

In contrast to sober Edinburgh Castle, Stirling's façade is festooned with all manner of weird, funny, and nude (if not rude) carvings. James V, who built the palace, had a liking for cherubs and demons. Most of the castle is 'only' about 500 years old – though the rock was fortified at least four centuries earlier. It is here that James III was born, his son and grandson, James IV and V, grew up, and Mary Queen of Scots was crowned.

church, which is lined by a three-tiered series of nine arches, is nearly intact. Also in Jedburgh is Mary Queen of Scots' House. This is a two-storey stone museum containing the queen's death warrant as well as a death mask, which was made just after her execution in 1587.

Both the museum and Jedburgh Abbey are open all the year round.

The Great Hall, which faces the upper square, was once the grandest Gothic chamber in Scotland – suitable for holding sessions of parliament – but it later suffered through two centuries of use as a military barracks. It is now in the process of being restored, but several superb sterling silver pieces may be seen in the banqueting section.

Among displays in the fine military museum are recruitment posters for the Argyll and Sutherland Highlanders, and two ramshead snuff boxes.

Until 1890, Stirling's **Auld Brig**, built of local stone in the 15th century, was the only span across the River Forth. You can still walk over it.

Visible to the south of the castle is the battlefield of **Bannockburn**. Here the National Trust presents an audio-visual show that clearly explains the complex wars of independence

Founded in 600, the cathedral of Dunblane still contains parts of the original building in its walls.

which culminated in Robert Bruce's epic victory over the English on this site in 1314. Commemorating this proud triumph for the Scots is a great greenish statue of Robert Bruce attired in chain-mail on horseback, together with the inscription of his declaration: 'We fight not for glory nor for wealth nor for honour, but only and alone we fight for freedom, which no good man surrenders but with his life'.

North of Stirling, 700-year-old **Dunblane Cathedral** is one of the finest examples of Gothic church architecture in Scotland. It is about a century older than **Doune Castle**, a few minutes' drive to the west, a fortress-residence also excellently preserved. Its owner, the Earl of Moray, displays his first-class collection of vintage cars at a nearby museum.

Romantically made popular by Sir Walter Scott in *Lady of*

the Lake and *Rob Roy*, the **Trossachs** is a region of lovely lochs and lochans, glens and bens. (It even includes Scotland's only 'lake', the attractive Lake of Menteith, which was a perfectly ordinary loch until last century when for some reason it began to be named in the English fashion.)

'Trossachs' probably means 'bristly places', after the area's wooded crags. It's easy to get off the beaten track here, since beaten tracks are few. Try the road past Loch Arklet to Inversnaid on Loch Lomond (a memorable dead-end), reached via the wild ravine country between Loch Katrine and Loch Achray, which is the core of the Trossachs. Salmon may well be leaping up the easily accessible falls of Leny below Loch Lubnaig.

Loch Lomond, the largest freshwater expanse in Great Britain, runs about 24 miles

*D*oune Castle was built in the 14th century and is now one of Scotland's best preserved ruins.

(39km) north to south. Most of its 30 isles and islets are privately owned. One has a good nature reserve. **Ben Lomond** (3,192ft/973m) looks down on the sometimes choppy water, as do several lesser peaks. **Luss** is probably the prettiest of the little lochside villages. From Balloch, the busiest, you can join excursions out to see the 'bonnie banks' aboard the *Countess Fiona*, a steamer which makes the trip to Inversnaid and back twice a day in the summer.

The tallest tree in Britain is alive, well and still growing at **Strone Garden** near Cairndow. With all its foliage, the top of this 188ft (57m) grand fir (*abies grandis*) cannot be seen. The giant has lots of lofty company in the garden's fine Pinetum.

Inveraray Castle, recovering from a serious fire in 1975, contains a wealth of treasures to fascinate visitors. Home of the dukes of Argyll, and situated west of Loch Fyne, it has been the headquarters of clan Campbell ('uncrowned kings of the Highlands') since the **41**

15th century, although the present building dates only from 1790. The armoury holds an amazing array of broadswords, Highland rifles, shields and medieval halberds in its collection of weaponry. The Turret Room's display of Wedgwood and other plate is stunning.

The guides point out with pride the castle's best portrait: that of the 6th Duke of Argyll.

It is said that not only did he gamble away £4 million, but he fathered 398 illegitimate children – which helps account for the 12 million Campbells around the world.

Further south along Loch Fyne, the delightful **Crarae Woodland Garden** has many shrubs of azaleas and rhododendrons as well as conifers. You can choose from three

walks over the 50 acres (20ha) of hillside, all within earshot of a plunging brook.

At the great Bronze and Stone Age archaeological area near Kilmartin, the best is hard to find: **Nether Largie North Cairn** is a ritual stone chamber used nearly 3,000 years ago. Clambering down, you will make out dozens of cup marks on the cover slab, along with carved axeheads which are thought to suggest Bronze-Age magic. Ask for directions to the track which leads to the cairn through sheep pastureland; it's not far from the sites of Nether Largie Cairn South and Templewood Stone Circle.

In this western area, warmed by the Gulf Stream, both exotic and sub-tropical plants flourish, particularly at **Arduaine Gardens**, on the coast below Kilmelford. Highlights include rare rhododendrons, azaleas and prize magnolias.

To the north of Oban, at Barcaldine, make time to visit the excellent **Oban Sealife Centre**, which has seals, a seal pup nursery and a hundred different marine species.

Further north again, **Glen Coe** knifes inland from Loch Leven through an impressive mountain range. The scenery, which boasts Highland sheep, red deer and golden eagles,

Loch Lomond – 'a sudden burst of prospect ... singular and beautiful'. (Dorothy Wordsworth) **43**

The china collection of Blair Castle is just one of the many priceless displays on view.

More often than not, clouds obscure the rounded summit of **Ben Nevis**, which, at 4,406ft (1,343m), is the highest mountain in Great Britain. The best view of the mountain is from the north, but it is most easily climbed from the west, starting near the bustling Highland touring centre of Fort William. Caution is advised here as bad weather closes in quickly at the top of Ben Nevis.

Inland, the long and thickly forested **Glen Garry** is one of Scotland's most wonderful mountain valleys. You'll understand Robert Burns' enthusiasm for the **Falls of Bruar** cascading into the River Garry near the lower end of the glen.

Blair Castle, just beyond, has put its little village of Blair Atholl on the map for countless excursion buses. Often reconstructed and restored, the white-turreted castle has long been the seat of the earls and dukes of Atholl. The present duke commands Britain's only 'private army', a ceremonial Highland regiment of about 60 local riflemen and 20 pipers and drummers who march in

attracts thousands of climbers and hikers. Geology, flora and fauna are illustrated at a visitor centre operated by the National Trust. In the steep valley, you'll find a memorial to the 1692 massacre of the Macdonalds. In bad weather, this is a bleak and even fearful place. A folk museum in the village of Glen Coe displays some **44** clan Macdonald paraphernalia.

their kilts very occasionally and haven't shot anybody for 170 years.

You can tour 32 rooms in the castle, part of which dates back 700 years. It's crammed with possessions amassed by the Atholl family over the centuries: an extensive china collection, swords, rifles, antlers, stuffed animals, and portraits everywhere. Look out in particular for two rare colonial American powder horns, one with a map carved on it that shows forts and settlements around Manhattan island, Albany and the Mohawk River.

A short drive to the south is the **Pass of Killiecrankie** where you will want to walk along wooded paths to the spectacular parts of the gorge. A National Trust centre here describes a particularly bloody battle between Jacobite and government forces in 1689.

Centrally located and proud of it, the crowded summer resort of **Pitlochry** is within reach of dozens of scenic and man-made attractions. In the town itself, you might visit the Pitlochry Dam and Fish Pass, where each year about 5,500 salmon are counted electronically and watched through a windowed chamber as they make their way towards their spawning grounds. The Pitlochry Festival Theatre is much frequented during its spring to autumn season.

To the west, a roadside promontory which is known as the **Queen's View** commands a glorious sweep down along Loch Tummel and over Highland hills. On a good day this is among the best panoramas in Scotland.

The delightful little village of **Fortingall**, with probably Scotland's finest thatched-roof cottages, has a past of history with mystery, and boasts the 'oldest living tree' in Europe. The hamlet rests in Glen Lyon, the 'longest, loveliest, loneliest' glen in Scotland, according to the locals. Tranquillity reigns. Tradition has it – without any scholarly confirmation – that Pontius Pilate was born in a nearby military encampment while his father was a Roman emissary to the Pictish king in the area.

There is no doubt, however, about the authenticity of the extremely ancient yew tree surrounded by a rusty iron and stone enclosure in Fortingall's churchyard. Still growing now, although reduced in size, the yew certainly doesn't look its presumed age – 3,000 years.

Don't miss **Dunkeld**, south of Pitlochry, with its splendidly restored 'little houses' from the 17th century. They lead to a grand, old cathedral which stands, partly ruined, amid tall trees, superior lawns and interesting gravestones beside the River Tay. St Columba is said to have preached in a monastery on this site. In Dunkeld's square is an information centre, and Thomas Telford's arched bridge (1809) over the Tay is much admired.

At the **Loch of the Lowes Wildlife Reserve**, two wooded miles from Dunkeld, you'll get an excellent opportunity to see an osprey. Binoculars are provided at a fine wooden hide where you can scan all kinds of water-bird life and study trees where ospreys nest after migrating from Africa.

At the hamlet **Meikleour**, 'one of the arboreal wonders of the world' lines the road: a gigantic beech hedge, which at about 90ft (27m) is the highest anywhere, planted in 1746 and patently thriving.

Enthusiasts of archaeology will appreciate the samples of elaborately carved early Christian and Pictish monuments in the museum at **Meigle**.

Just north of Perth, acres of green lawns surround the pale, red sandstone of **Scone Palace**, as historic a site as any in Scotland. Here all, or nearly all, the kings of the Scots were crowned on the Stone of Destiny, which Edward I vengefully took away from Scone (pronounced 'Scoon') in 1296 and brought to London. (Some believe the stone now incorporated in the Coronation Chair in Westminster Abbey, London is not the original Stone, which dated to the 9th century, but a replica produced by the Scots for Edward to seize. Romantics suggest the real stone is still hidden in Scotland.)

To reach this ancestral home of the earls of Mansfield you

will proceed past some temperamental peacocks. The best pieces of furniture are French, and the china includes early Sèvres, Derby and Meissen. In the Long Gallery are more than 80 Vernis Martin objects which look just like lacquered porcelain but are in fact *papier mâché*. This unique collection will never be duplicated: the Martin brothers died in Paris in the 18th century without disclosing the secret of their varnish. Before leaving Scone, stroll through the grounds to the Pinetum, an imposing col-

Scone Palace – handsome but unassuming – is one of Scotland's invaluable gems.

lection of California sequoias, cedars, Norway spruces, silver firs and other conifers in a gorgeous setting.

Glamis Castle, yet another stately Scottish pile, lies northeast of Perth towards Forfar. It was the childhood home of Queen Elizabeth the Queen Mother and the birthplace of **47**

Princess Margaret, and visitors can take guided tours through the magnificent rooms which contain fine paintings, furniture and porcelain.

South, on the Firth of Tay, lies **Dundee**, famous maritime and industrial centre, the home of marmalade, and birthplace of *Dennis the Menace* and many other children's comic characters. The town is now dusting down its heavy-duty industrial image and invites visitors to take a closer look.

Top of the list of attractions is Captain Scott's ship the *Discovery*, built in the city at the turn of the century. Alongside,

at **Discovery Point**, Scott's adventures are brought to life with displays, videos and the use of special effects.

The city's **MacManus Galleries** has a very good late-19th-century art collection and includes works by Millet and Rossetti. The paintings are all displayed in a reconstructed Victorian gallery.

On the Fife coast, **St Andrews** is inevitably busy, since it is known worldwide as the home of golf. Here the game of golf has been played for 500 years. Anyone can tee off on the Old Course at the Royal and Ancient Golf Club, where so many championships have been held (see p.87-88). This pleasant seaside resort is home to Scotland's oldest university (founded in 1411) and has the ruin of Scotland's largest-ever cathedral, built in the 12th and 13th centuries, where the marriage of James V and Mary of Guise was held. An escape-proof 'bottle dungeon' is in the town's castle. The local theatre is well regarded, and there is a bi-annual arts festival.

Picturesque fishing villages on Fife's south-eastern coast, called East Neuk, are favoured by holidaymakers as well as golfers. **Crail**, where you're likeliest to find freshly caught lobster, is a quaint little port with a Dutch-style Tolbooth (court-house-jail) tower and restored buildings which are a photographer's delight.

Anstruther (which the locals pronounce 'Anster'), once the herring capital of Scotland, is worth a stop for its **Scottish Fisheries Museum**, with its realistic fisherman's cottage of about 1900, magnificent ship models, whale tusks and display about trawlers. From here

you can go to the Isle of May, a bird sanctuary with cliffs that measure 250ft (76m).

Down at **Pittenweem**, another venerable fishing harbour, you often see masses of shrimp among the seafood brought in by the fleet to the thriving quayside market.

*F*ishermen have been bringing in the catch at Crail (left) in north-east Fife for centuries.

49

The North East

The term 'granite city' is self-explanatory when you see the buildings sparkling in the sunshine at **Aberdeen**.

Surprisingly, however, this solid metropolis, further north than Moscow, is anything but sombre: roses, daffodils and crocuses flourish in such profusion that the town has won the Britain-in-Bloom trophy a record ten times.

(You will find Aberdeen's excellent tourist information centre at St Nicholas House on Broad Street.)

Scotland's third city (pop. 210,000) is Great Britain's third largest fishing port, and that means the best show in town. Don't fail to make an early morning visit (best about 7.30am) to the huge harbourside **fish market**. Containers of fish by the thousand are unloaded from the weathered trawlers. There are huge triangular halibut, long black-grey 'coaleys' (coalfish), gigantic skate, greyish-white ling, dogfish, turbot, whiting, cod, haddock and many other edible denizens of the North Sea. You'll see them iced, hauled, counted, bought and carried off by hearty Aberdonians.

Even though the traditional fishing industry is thriving, it is not the reason why Aberdeen today is Scotland's boom

*G*et to grips with the 'real' Aberdeen by visiting the harbour when the fleet comes in.

city. Most of the boats arriving in the harbour service the great oil rigs out to sea beyond the horizon. Ashore, the city's facilities have swelled to accommodate the influx of North Sea oil personnel, creating a rather odd international atmosphere for the thousands of tourists who arrive in the summer.

Touring Aberdeen you will inevitably see **Marischal College**, the second largest granite building in the world. Right in the heart of town, it is built of a lighter-coloured variety known as 'white granite' and forms part of the complex of Aberdeen University.

The other part is **King's College**, a much less granitic campus, a short drive away in mostly medieval Old Aberdeen. Dominating the pleasant quadrangle is the beloved local landmark, the Crown Tower of King's Chapel. Knocked down in a storm in 1633, the structure was rebuilt with Renaissance additions. Inside the chapel, look for the arched oak ceiling and the carved screen and stalls, outstanding medieval woodwork.

Nearby you walk through a crowded graveyard to the oldest cathedral in Aberdeen, **St Machar**, first built in 1357, but rebuilt mostly in granite in the following century, it is described by scholarly guides as the 'most remarkable fortified cathedral in western Europe'. Capping the marvellous stone interior with its stained-glass windows is another oak ceiling bearing seals of kings and religious leaders.

Aside from the cathedral, nothing of note was built of granite until about 200 years ago. Today half of Aberdeen's granite buildings came from **Rubislaw Quarry**, which was opened in 1741 and finally ran out of stone in 1970. What remains is a mammoth hole, which is situated surprisingly close to the centre of Aberdeen out along Queens Road. Now fenced off and overgrown, Rubislaw is awesome.

The 17th-century **Mercat Cross**, which is ringed by a parapet on which are engraved the names of Scottish monarchs from James I to James VII, is claimed to be the finest **51**

The gardens at Crathes Castle are among the most spectacular in the country.

example of a burgh (chartered town) cross to survive in Scotland. Aberdeen has in fact been a burgh for a long time: it received a charter in 1179 from William the Lion.

The long, picturesque valley of the **River Dee**, which extends inland from Aberdeen to the high Cairngorm Mountains, has been called Royal Deeside since Queen Victoria **52** wrote glowingly about the

area. She often holidayed at **Balmoral Castle** after Prince Albert, her consort, bought the huge estate in 1852 and refashioned the turreted mansion in accordance with his own taste. The granite is local and lighter than Aberdeen's. From May 1 to July 31, if the royal family is not using Balmoral, the grounds are open to the public. Across the road, the modest **Crathie Church** is attended by the royal family, but is unspoiled despite being an inevitable tourist attraction.

Further along the Dee in the direction of Aberdeen **Crathes Castle** has some of Scotland's most dramatic gardens, with giant yew hedges which are clipped just once a year by gardeners who are obviously skilled in the art. The views from within the 16th-century tower house over these remarkable hedges are in themselves worth the visit. Look also for the three rooms with painted ceilings, the carved oak ceiling in the top floor gallery and the 14th-century ivory Horn of Leys, which is above the drawing-room fireplace.

South east, a short distance away from Stonehaven, the vast ruins of **Dunottar Castle** rise imposingly above the sea. The fortress has had a rich and varied history. Here, in 1297, William Wallace burned alive an English Plantagenet garrison, while much later, in 1650, the Scottish Crown Regalia was kept here during a siege by Oliver Cromwell's Roundheads. More recently, not to mention more peacefully, the film director Franco Zeffirelli used Dunottar as the location for his film of *Hamlet*. Note: the steep steps leading down to the castle may be difficult for less mobile visitors.

At Pitmedden, to the north of Aberdeen, the rare 17th-century **formal garden** covers 3 sunken acres (1¼ha). Some 37,000 plants form elaborate designs, patterned after those of Edinburgh's Holyroodhouse Palace and set off by clipped box hedges and shaven lawns.

On the often stormy coast south of Peterhead, you may have to ask for directions to the **Bullers of Buchan**, near Cruden Bay. These are plunging, wildly beautiful clefts in the rugged high sea-cliffs with the screams of marine birds echoing up from the caverns. Note that these cliffs are dangerous, and it can be slippery along the narrow pathways out to one of the most gorgeous, dramatic spots in Scotland.

Nearby, unmarked, down a bumpy track from the village Cruden Bay, are the impressive, reddish ruins of **Slains Castle**. On fine days the green cliffs below the castle are a perfect spot for a picnic. On the other hand, if the mist is blowing in from the sea and swirling around the ruins, you will appreciate the literary associations the castle has had with Dracula.

West of Fraserburgh are two of Scotland's tiniest, most appealing fishing villages, **Pennan** and **Crovie**. A precipitous road twists in hairpin bends down to Pennan's trim, white, twin-chimneyed houses on a small bay. You will find that visitors are greeted with great friendliness by the fisherfolk who live on this little-known part of the coast.

The Highlands

No longer really remote, the happily under-populated north of Scotland offers above all superb scenery, but also the country's most amusing castle, most mysterious monster and most delightful distilleries.

Just about everywhere is reached via **Inverness**, capital of the Highlands since the days of the ancient Picts. Unless it's Sunday, stop for an hour in this busy town to tour the small, modern **Museum and Art Gallery** in Castle Wynd. In a fascinating exhibition of Scottish Highland history dating back to the Stone Age, you can brush up your clan lore as well as see dirks and sporrans, broadswords and powder horns.

Strategically sited where the River Ness joins the Moray Firth, Inverness is not at all shy about exploiting the submarine

celebrity presumed to inhabit the waters of **Loch Ness** to the south. 'Nessie' T-shirts and all kinds of 'monster' bric-à-brac are on sale. Excursion boats make regular monster-spotting cruises and there is now a submarine trip which lowers you to the bed of the lake for a somewhat murky view (contact the Scottish Tourist Board for details, see p.126). A careful count is kept of Nessie sightings: in recent times more than a dozen a year have been

The Highlands are an outdoors place: visit moody Loch Ness, or bag a few grouse.

considered reliable – and there have also been some very persuasive photographs.

With sonar and underwater cameras now apparently closing in on the mystery, most of the experts involved seem to agree that not one, but a number of large aquatic creatures roam the very murky depths of Loch Ness, surviving by eating eels and other fish. Seven rivers feed this loch, bringing in millions of peat particles which reduce visibility to zero

below 40ft (12m). At 23 miles (37km) long and about a mile (1.6km) across, Loch Ness is generally about 700ft (213m) deep – though in one area the silted bottom is nearly 1,000ft (305m). That means enough space for large families of the monster which has intrigued people ever since it was first reported in the 6th century – by no less revered a traveller than St Columba.

About 5 miles (8km) east of Inverness at **Culloden Moor**, Jacobite headstones, a mini-museum and an information centre recall the 1746 victory of Cumberland's redcoats over Bonnie Prince Charlie's Highlanders – the last major battle fought on UK soil. The young prince's adventures are retold in a stirring 15-minute film.

Near the battlefield is the impressive archaeological site of **Clava Cairns**. Three once domed tombs are encircled by

*C*awdor Castle, the home of the Cawdor family, dates from 1372, but has a tree that's older.

standing stones. To stand in a silent burial chamber dating back to 1800 BC and 1500 BC is a fascinating, awesome and slightly eerie experience.

'Three out of four Ghosts prefer **Cawdor Castle**' proclaims the sign at the castle's authentic drawbridge entrance. This is the only castle in Scotland which keeps you laughing as you learn. Don't fail to read the signs that describe what you're seeing. They will keep you from brooding about the fact that in this fortress home of the earls of Cawdor, Shakespeare had Duncan murdered by Macbeth.

For your safety, you'll have to forego the tempting spiral steps up to the tower which has survived since 1454. The tower's **Thorn Tree Room** is a stone vault enclosing a 600-year-old Hawthorn tree. The castle grounds have outstanding flower and kitchen gardens, a nature trail and even a pitch-and-putt course. Then head for nearby **Cawdor village**, where the stone cottages, the cemetery and even the cows are delightful.

For salmon and whisky, Scotland can offer you nothing better than the **River Spey**. Driving along this beautiful valley of ferns and old bridges you'll want to stop to watch anglers casting their long lines into this fastest-flowing river in the British Isles and, often enough, hauling in a shimmering salmon. Nestling among

*Y*ou'll see several barrelsful on the whisky trail; coopers are vital to the whisky-ageing process.

the trees are slate-roofed buildings with pagoda chimneys. Here they produce the finest of all the fine Scotch whiskies, or so the local enthusiasts insist.

In this area, what is promoted as the world's only **whisky trail** takes in four or more distilleries where you can watch malt being distilled by a process that has remained basically unchanged for 500 years. You will usually be invited to enjoy a free wee dram. Local tourist offices know which are the distilleries that accommodate visitors and when they're

closed for maintenance (annual shutdowns last up to six weeks, often in July-August). If you're lucky, in the cooperage you'll see a cooper (cask maker) fashioning oak staves into a cask: by law a spirit can't be called 'whisky' until it has been aged in oak for three years. According to the experts, the best maturity for Scotch is about ten years.

Around the malt centre of **Dufftown** they still like to quote the saying: 'Rome was built on seven hills, Dufftown stands on seven stills' – although at a recent count there were in fact eight distilleries.

At Carrbridge the popular **Landmark Visitor Centre** features a multi-screen film about the history of the Highlands, a nature trail and an exhibition of modern sculpture in a woodland setting.

Aviemore is probably the most elaborate and modern holiday centre in Scotland, and is open all winter for skiing in the nearby mountains. On a clear and not too windy day, take an exhilarating chair-lift ride up into the high Cairngorms where rangers lead conducted walks.

Seven miles (11km) south, the excellent **Highland Wildlife Park** at Kincraig has a drive-through area (don't leave your car, and close the windows if animals approach). It may remind you of a game park in Kenya – except of course for the radically different wildlife. You should see all or most of these animals living wild or semi-wild: red deer, Highland cattle, ibex, Przewalski's wild horses, soay sheep, European bison and mouflon (forebears of domestic sheep). Stars of the walk-through section include arctic foxes, bears and wildcats.

Moving west from Inverness to the coast, the dramatic **Loch Torridon** area is well-known for its mountains of red-brown sandstone and white quartzite. The charming and peaceful lochside hamlet of **Shieldaig**, opposite a nature reserve islet, may tempt you to tarry awhile.

The Gulf Stream works its warming magic again at **Inverewe Gardens**, a colourful **59** subtropical oasis overlooking Loch Ewe on the same latitude as Juneau, Alaska. Late spring and early summer are the best seasons to visit the gardens, whose highlights include some giant magnolias and the exotic Himalayan Hound's Tooth.

At a fine wooded spot just a minute's walk off the highway below Loch Broom are the **Falls of Measach**, plunging 200ft (61m) into the awesome Corrieshalloch Gorge. These falls are worth a long look from the suspension bridge.

Scotland's most memorable scenery lies probably along the jagged **north-west coast** above **Ullapool**, a little fishing port doubling as ferry terminal for the Outer Hebrides. Whenever possible, take the secondary roads closest to the shore. You will wind through truly beautiful country filled with mossy rocks, ferns and hundreds of tiny lochans. The first section goes through the Inverpolly Nature Reserve.

Strange stories are recounted about gorgeous **Suilven**, the mount looming over the wild landscape near to Lochinver

(why don't animals graze on its slopes?). During the summer an excursion boat sets out from tiny Tarbet to **Handa Island**, a teeming bird sanctuary with huge sandstone cliffs and sandy beaches.

You can reach the Scottish mainland's north-western extremity, **Cape Wrath**, by ferry and minibus in the summer. Go on a clear day – from the towering cliffs here the birdwatching and seascape are superb. This area of Scotland also contains some of the oldest rocks in the world.

Near the friendly hamlet of Durness, **Smoo Cave** has a beautiful setting at the end of a dramatic sea inlet. The 'gloophole' through the cathedral-like limestone roof of the large outer cavern gets its name from the noise of air rushing up through it at high tide. Without venturing inside the second cave, you can photograph its 80ft (24m) waterfall from the entrance.

At the end of World War II, some German submarines put into deep and scenic **Loch Eriboll** to surrender to the

Royal Navy. Further east, the coastal scenery around the **Kyle of Tongue** is glorious.

A lighthouse with stout red foghorns stands on **Dunnet Head**, a windy promontory on the northernmost point in the Scottish mainland, overlooking a forbidding sea. Sheep graze here, birds swoop past, and if there's no mist, Orkney is visible on the horizon.

Nearby **John O'Groats** is far better known, although it isn't quite the most northern end of Great Britain. The sign here declares it is 874 miles (1,406km) to Land's End in Cornwall, the greatest overland distance between any two points in Britain.

Duncansby Head close by, with its clifftop lighthouse, is the most north-easterly point. Be warned that if the foghorn blows while you're here, you won't soon forget it. Offshore the unusual pillar-like Stacks

---

Kilts and Tartans

For the Scotsman, Highland dress is not just an item of folklore to be brought out on ceremonial occasions. It's everyday wear for some, and uniform of certain regiments. You'll probably see at least one pipe and drum band arrayed in kilted splendour.

Day-time Highland dress consists of a knee-length kilt, matching vest and tweed jacket, long knitted hose (with a knife stuck in the right stocking) and garters. A sporran (purse) hangs from the waist, and a plaid (sort of tartan rug) is sometimes flung over the shoulder.

Authentic tartans are registered designs. Each clan – originally an organization based on a family – had its own pattern. As the clans subdivided, many variations (setts) of the tartans were produced. Today, it is estimated that there are more than a thousand. Although a certain amount of commercialism surrounds the tartan business, you may have a genuine clan association – even if your family name seems far removed from Campbell, Macdonald or Stewart.

of Duncansby make a good photograph.

Inland and quite a way to the south, make a short detour from the angling centre of Lairg to **Shin Falls** where, with luck, you'll see sizeable salmon leaping up low, churning falls along the river.

The South West

GLASGOW

In recent years, Glasgow has undergone major changes, and has risen to become one of the UK's leading tourist destinations. Be prepared for a pleasant surprise: the city has not only cleaned its splendid Victorian buildings and generally polished up its act but now proudly presents itself as one of Europe's major centres for culture and the arts. It is home to the Scottish National Opera, Ballet and Orchestra, and has a bustling arts and theatre scene, including the annual arts festival, Mayfest.

At the heart of Glasgow **62** lies **George Square**, which is overlooked by the august **City Chambers**. You can catch a city bus tour from here in the summer, and just round the corner in St Vincent Place, you will find the Tourist Information Centre (due to move to George Square in April 1996).

From the city centre you can take a bus to one of Glasgow's major sights, the **Burrell Collection**, a spectacular museum opened in 1983. Set in Pollok Park, an innovative building was specially commissioned to hold the thousands of pieces amassed earlier this century by Scottish shipping tycoon Sir William Burrell. The collection includes all kinds of things – from ancient Greek statues to Impressionist paintings – with medieval tapestries and stained glass being among its prize exhibits. It also has a Rembrandt self-portrait and a number of works by Degas.

Also in Pollok Park is **Pollok House** which has a fine collection of Spanish art.

In Kelvingrove Park is the city's splendid **Art Gallery and Museum**. On display here are Rembrandt's *A Man In Ar-*

mour, Van Gogh's *Portrait of Alexander Reid*, Giorgione's *The Adulteress Brought Before Christ*, and Bellini's *The Madonna with the Child Blessing*. The Gallery also has good French Impressionist and Post-Impressionist paintings, and works by the Glasgow Boys and Scottish colourists.

The **Transport Museum** has the world's oldest bicycle.

An outstanding feature of Glasgow's urban landscape is the series of beautiful Art Nouveau buildings designed by Scottish architect **Charles Rennie Mackintosh**. Still in use, the **Glasgow School of Art**, off Sauchiehall Street, is considered to be his supreme architectural achievement, and is open on weekdays and Saturdays. On Sauchiehall Street, stop off at the Mackintosh-designed **Willow Tearooms**,

The statue of Sir Walter Scott in George Square was the first to be dedicated to him (1837).

located on the first floor above Henderson's jewellers. From May to September 1996, a Charles Rennie Mackintosh exhibition will be held down the road at the McLellan Galleries, with over 300 works on display. A number of guided tours are also organised by the Charles Rennie Mackintosh Society. (For further information, call 0141 946 6600.)

The **Tenement House**, just a short walk away, is a restored Victorian tenement flat, which reveals what life was like in a typical Glasgow home at the turn of the century.

Glasgow's main shopping area is back towards George Square and focuses on Buchanan and Argyle streets. If you feel like spending money – or just browsing – pop into **Princes Square**, where there are some of Glasgow's most sophisticated designer shops.

To the north east of the city centre stands Glasgow's fine, if somewhat grim-faced, medieval **cathedral**. In parts almost 800 years old, it contains the tomb of St Mungo, the city's patron saint.

The area surrounding the cathedral has been extensively renovated, and here you can visit the **Provand's Lordship House**, the oldest house in Glasgow, as well as the recently-opened **St Mungo Museum of Religious Life and Art**. Dedicated to the importance of religion in human life, St Mungo's has in its collection Salvador Dali's extraordinary *Crucifixion*, and a magnificent bronze image of the Hindu goddess Shiva.

Behind the cathedral is the **Necropolis**, which holds the extravagantly-styled tombs of the city's late, great Victorians.

If you want to get a feel for the 'real' culture and people of Glasgow, head eastwards to **Glasgow Green**, one of the city's many public parks and the oldest in Britain. Here you can discover a little about the working life of Glaswegians over the years in the fascinating **People's Palace**.

Open at weekends, the nearby **Barras** street market will give you the chance to rub shoulders with local people and pick up a bargain or two.

64

A Selection of
Scottish Hotels
and Restaurants

Recommended Hotels

Accommodation around Scotland covers a wide spectrum, from the basic B & B (Bed and Breakfast) to modern luxury hotels and ancient refurbished castles. The Scottish Tourist Board (see p.126) publishes many brochures and booklets detailing the types of accommodation available, prices, facilities and so on.

Below you will find a selection of hotels divided into three categories, all chosen for their price and quality of accommodation. Prices are based on one person sharing a double room for one night, with breakfast, and the categories give a rough guide to what you might expect to pay, but bear in mind that time of year and availability will influence pricing. Edinburgh is extremely busy during the International Festival (September), so book well in advance if you plan to visit the capital during that period. The hotels are listed in alphabetical order.

‖‖‖	£100-180
‖‖	£50-100
‖	below £50

Ardsheal House ‖‖‖
Kentallen, Highland, PA38 4BX
Tel. (063174) 227
fax (063174) 342
Historic house in lochside setting 17 miles (27km) from Fort William, offering good food and tennis. Open all week from Easter to November, and for weekends and holidays in the winter. 13 rooms.

Arisaig House ‖‖‖
Beasdale, Arisaig,
Inverness-shire, PH39 4NR
Tel. (06875) 622
fax (06875) 626

Fine hotel in an old mansion above Loch nan Uamh, 3 miles (5km) south east of Arisaig on A830. Croquet. Excellent food. Closed November to March. 14 rooms.

Banchory Lodge ‖‖
Banchory, Kincardineshire,
AB31 3HS
Tel. (0330) 822625
fax (0330) 825019
Family-run hotel set in a Georgian country house. Traditional Scottish home cooking. Fishing, sauna. Closed 26-27 December and first week in January.

Cairn Hotel   ‖

10-18 Windsor Street,
Edinburgh, EH7 5JR
Tel. 031 557 0175
fax 031 556 8221

Medium-size hotel located on the eastern edge of Edinburgh city centre. Colour TV in all rooms. Friendly atmosphere. 75 rooms.

Caledonian Hotel   ‖‖

Princes Street, Edinburgh,
EH1 2AB
Tel. 031 225 2433
fax 031 225 6632

Old-style luxury hotel at western end of bustling Princes Street in the shadow of Edinburgh Castle. French and Scottish menus. Some rooms are adapted for disabled visitors. 240 rooms.

Caledonian Thistle   ‖

10, Union Terrace,
Aberdeen, AB9 1HE
Tel. (0224) 640233
fax (0224) 311162

Centrally located Victorian building with modern facilities, own restaurant and café/wine bar. Executive rooms. Sauna. 80 rooms.

Ceilidh Place   ‖-‖

14 West Argyle Street,
Ullapool, IV26 2TY
Tel. (0854) 612103
fax (0854) 612886

Small, friendly hotel with popular restaurant, bar and coffee shop, it also stages musical performances and art exhibitions. 24 rooms.

Channings Hotel   ‖

South Learmonth Gardens,
Edinburgh, EH4 1EZ
Tel. 031 315 2226
fax 031 332 9631

Comfortable hotel on quiet Georgian Terrace. Convenient for Edinburgh city centre. Brasserie, bar and patio garden. 48 rooms.

Culloden House   ‖‖

Culloden, Inverness, IV1 2NZ
Tel. (0463) 790461
fax (0463) 792181

Georgian house close to the site of the 1746 battle, and 3 miles (5km) east of Inverness on the A96. Facilities include tennis, sauna and solarium. Restaurant. 20 rooms.

Dalmunzie House   ‖

Spittal of Glenshee,
Tayside, PH10 7QG
Tel. (0250) 885224
fax (0250) 885225

A mountain lodge with splendid views, situated 18 miles (29km) north of Blairgowrie on the A93. Good home cooking on offer as well as fishing, golf and tennis. Conveniently located for the ski slopes. 16 rooms.

One Devonshire Gardens ||||

1 Devonshire Gardens,
Glasgow, G12 0UX
Tel. 041 339 2001
fax 041 337 1663

Located in a leafy western suburb of Glasgow, this luxury hotel has been adapted from Victorian mansion houses. Fine creative restaurant. 27 rooms.

Farleyer House ||

Weem, Aberfeldy,
Perthshire, PH15 2JE
Tel. (0887) 820332
fax (0887) 829430

Country house hotel on B846, 1 mile (1.6km) west of Weem near Loch Tay. Restaurant and bistro. Golf, gardens and use of facilities at nearby Elliott Country Club. Closed first fortnight in January. 11 rooms.

Greywalls ||||

Duncar Road, Muirfield, Gullane,
East Lothian, EH31 2EG
Tel. (0620) 842144;
fax (0620) 842241

Attractive Lutyens house with Jekyll Gardens, fine views and a good restaurant, located 40 minutes' drive from the centre of Edinburgh. Golf, tennis and croquet on offer. Closed from November to March. 22 rooms.

Forte Crest ||

Bothwell St, Glasgow, G2 7EN
Tel. 041 248 2656
fax 041 221 8986

Modern high-rise hotel in central location with commanding views over the city. Two restaurants and bar. Office services available.

Inverlochy Castle ||||

Torlundy, Inverness-shire,
PH33 5BN
Tel. (0397) 702177
fax (0397) 702953

Luxury Victorian castle 3 miles (5km) north east of Fort William on A82. Set in 50 acres of woodland with splendid views of the loch and mountains. Fine cuisine, tennis, fishing. Closed mid-November to mid-March. 16 rooms.

Kildrummy Castle ||

Kildrummy, Alford,
Grampian, AAB3 8RA
Tel. (09755) 71288
fax (09755) 71345

Country house in baronial castle style near the old castle ruins and Kildrummy Gardens. Snooker, fishing, Closed January. 15 rooms.

Kingsmills Hotel ||

Culcabock Road, Inverness,
IV2 3LP
Tel. (0463) 237166;
fax (0463) 225208

Set in landscaped gardens. Golf, indoor swimming pool, gym, sauna, solarium, hair and beauty salons. Restaurant. Villas in hotel grounds also available. 79 rooms.

Knockinaam Lodge ▌▌

Portpatrick, Dumfries and
Galloway, DG9 9AD
Tel. (077681) 471
fax (077681) 435
Victorian Lodge Hotel set in beautiful parkland. Fine sea views, excellent food, fishing and croquet. Closed from January until just before Easter.

Marriott Hotel ▌▌

500 Argyle Street, Glasgow,
G12 0UX
Tel. 041 226 5577
fax 041 221 9202
Central, high-rise hotel. Indoor swimming pool, sauna, solarium and squash. Bistro-style and formal restaurants, café-bar. Photocopying, fax service, etc. also available. 300 rooms.

The Peat Inn ▌▌▌

Peat Inn, by Cupar, Fife,
KY15 5LH
Tel. (033484) 206
fax (033484) 530
Hostelry 6 miles (10km) southeast of Cupar on B940. Excellent restaurant (see p.71). 8 rooms.

Roxburghe Hotel ▌▌

38 Charlotte Square, Edinburgh,
EH42 4HG
Tel. 031 225 3921
fax 031 220 2518
Traditional style hotel overlooking elegant Charlotte Square. Only one minute from Princes Street. Restaurant and bistro. 75 rooms.

Rufflets ▌▌

Strathkinness Low Road,
St Andrews, Fife, KY16 9TX
Tel. (0334) 72594
fax (0334) 78703
Country house set in its own splendid gardens, offering good Scottish home cooking. 25 rooms.

St Andrews Old Course Hotel ▌▌▌

St Andrews, Fife, KY16 9SP
Tel. (0334) 74371
fax (0334) 77668
Modern luxury hotel adjoining the historic golf course, with good restaurants, indoor swimming pool, health spa and beauty salon.

Sunlaws House ▌▌

Heiton, Kelso, TD5 8JZ
Tel. (0573) 450331
fax (0573) 450611
Victorian country mansion 3 miles (5 km) south-west of Kelso. Good cuisine, tennis, clayshooting, croquet and fishing 22 rooms.

Recommended Restaurants

The restaurants in this section are listed alphabetically for ease of reference. Prices quoted are per person and include starter, mid-priced main course and dessert, but not wine, coffee or service.

We have noted the times when the restaurants plan to be closed, but it is always a good idea to check before you turn up. Many of the restaurants listed below are very popular and you will usually need to book your table in advance to avoid being disappointed, especially in the bigger towns and cities.

Vegetarianism has not taken off in Scotland to quite the same extent as in England, so vegetarian restaurants are rather thin on the ground. However, many places now offer at least one vegetarian dish per course, but check what's likely to be on offer before you book.

▮▮▮	above £30
▮▮	£15-30
▮	below £15

L'Auberge ▮▮

56 St Mary's Street,
Edinburgh, EH1 1SX
Tel. 031 556 5888
Inventive French-style cuisine in elegant surroundings and noted for seafood, game and desserts.Close to Edinburgh's Royal Mile. Closed 26 December and 1 January.

Café Gandolfi ▮-▮▮

64 Albion St, Glasgow G1
Tel. 041 552 6813
Set in the heart of Glasgow's merchant city, it offers coffees, teas, lunches and evening meals in a beautifully designed interior.

Champany Inn ▮▮▮

Champany, Linlithgow,
West Lothian, EH49 7LU
Tel. (050683) 4532
Acclaimed for its steaks and wine cellar, it is set in an old mill, with beamed ceilings and antique tables. An informal, moderately priced 'Chop and Ale House' adjoins it. Booking advised.

Fouter's Bistro ▮-▮▮

2a Academy Street, Ayr
Tel. 0292 261391
Located in the cellars of an old bank, this informal restaurant offers hearty portions of fine Scot-

tish produce prepared in a French style. A favourite in summer is the well-priced lobster lunch. Vegetarians and special diets catered for. Closed Sunday, Monday, 25-27 December and 1-4 January. Booking strongly advised.

The Kalpna

2-3 St Patrick Square,
Edinburgh, EH8 9EZ
Tel. 031 667 9890

Enjoy excellent vegetarian dishes in this subtly decorated, Indian restaurant situated on the south side of the city. Non-smoking. Closed Saturday lunchtime and Sunday. Open every day during the Edinburgh Festival when advance booking is essential.

Loch Fyne Oyster Bar

Clachan Farm, Cairndow,
Argyll PA26 8BH
Tel. (04996) 264

Inauspicious-looking restaurant at the top of Loch Fyne which serves excellent fish and seafood dishes. Simple but cosy decor with pine tables and white-painted walls. An adjoining shop sells seafood and local produce. Booking advised.

Martin's

70 Rose Street, North Lane,
Edinburgh EH2 3DX
Tel. 031 225 3106

Small, cosy, family-run restaurant in the heart of Edinburgh. Inventive menu. Closed Saturday lunch, Sunday, Monday, 4 weeks before Christmas and 10 days in June and September. Booking advised.

Owlies Brasserie

Unit 3, Littlejohn Street, Aberdeen
Tel. 0224 649267

Spacious warehouse-style restaurant close to Marischal College, serving French country cooking in an informal atmosphere. Serves both snacks and full meals. Vegetarian menu. Closed Sunday, Monday and Christmas/New Year.

La Parmigiana

447 Great Western Road,
Glasgow, G12 8HH
Tel. 041 334 0686

Small, family-run establishment in Glasgow's west end, serves fresh, authentic Italian cuisine in elegant surroundings. Closed Sunday.

The Peat Inn

Peat Inn, by Cupar,
Fife, KY15 5LH
Tel. (033484) 206

Situated 6 miles (10km) south of Cupar on the B940, this celebrated restaurant specializes in cuisine using fresh local produce, especially seafood, in a delightful country-style setting. Closed 25 **71**

December and 1 January. A few luxury rooms available (see p.69).

Pierre Victoire's   I-II

10 Victoria Street, Edinburgh,
EH1 2HG
Tel. 031 225 1721

Lively and sometimes chaotic bistro-style restaurant just off the Royal Mile, offering good quality food with a French influence. The popular lunchtime set menu offers a bargain three courses for just over £5. Part of a franchise, you will find other branches in Edinburgh as well as Glasgow, Aberdeen, Inverness, Perth and Ayr. Booking recommended.

Rogano's   III

11 Exchange Place, Glasgow G1
Tel. 041 248 4055

Opened in 1935, the restaurant's art deco interior is in the same style as the *Queen Mary*, under construction on the Clyde at the time. Just off Buchanan Street, it specializes in seafood. More informal, moderately priced restaurant downstairs. Booking essential.

The Shore   II

3 The Shore, Edinburgh,
EH6 6QW
Tel. 031 553 5080

Informal restaurant with delightful decor, offering excellent seafood in waterfront setting. Live jazz in the adjoining bar, usually at the weekend. Booking recommended.

The Silver Darlings   II-III

Pocra Quay, Footdec, Aberdeen
Tel. 0224 576229

A stylish harbourside restaurant specializing in seafood barbecue. Booking recommended, especially at weekends. Closed from 24 December to 6 January.

The Ubiquitous Chip   III

12 Ashton Lane, Glasgow G12
Tel. 041 334 5007

Just off Byres Road in Glasgow's west end, the 'Chip' serves Scottish food in leafy courtyard surroundings. The lively bar upstairs is renowned for its wines and beers, and also offers more moderately priced meals. Booking is highly recommended.

Whitecross   II-III

Ivy Cottage, Muirtown Locks,
Inverness
Tel. 0463 240386

Set in a cottage on the banks of the Caledonian canal and serving high-quality Scottish dishes with a French twist. Good selection of wines. Vegetarian meals. Closed Sunday, Monday, Saturday lunch and the first two weeks of November and January. Booking advised.

ARRAN

Surprisingly unspoilt, the isle of Arran in the Firth of Clyde has beautiful scenery as well as all the atmosphere of the Scottish Highlands and islands. Car ferries ply regularly between Arran's capital Brodick and Ardrossan on the Ayrshire coast; the journey takes 55 minutes. During summer a smaller ferry links northern Arran to Claonaig in Argyll.

Brodick village nestles on a bay in the shadow of **Goatfell**, which, at 2,866ft (874m), is the highest peak on Arran, and forms a complete contrast to Glasgow's suburban sprawl. Red deer roam wild around the island's beautiful mountain glens and can often be seen in North Glen Sannox between Lochranza and Sannox.

Arran is above all, however, an island for hill walkers or climbers. There are ten summits over 2,000ft (610m) and dozens of ridge routes. Among the hundred or so species of bird known to frequent Arran are peregrine falcons and rare golden eagles, and seals like the rocks around Arran's 56 miles (90km) of coast. In addition, basking sharks are seen offshore in the summer. Arran has some outstanding archaeological sites including Neolithic chamber tombs.

In the midst of grounds full of rhododendrons, azaleas and roses stands **Brodick Castle**, open from Easter to October. The castle contains a wealth of treasures and is surrounded by magnificent gardens.

The most dramatic scenery to be found on Arran is to the north. In the south the topography is gentler, with pleasant hills around the villages of Lamlash and Whiting Bay.

Towards the island's southwest corner on a wild, cliff-backed coast are the **King's Caves**, where Robert Bruce is said to have watched a spider try and try again – which taught him how to deal with Scotland's destiny. They are a 20-minute walk from the place where you leave the car. The cathedral-like main cave of yellow, green and grey rock has a creaking iron gate to keep out wandering sheep. **73**

No human habitation is in sight, and nothing seems to disturb the birds diving into the sea for fish.

DUMFRIES AND GALLOWAY

Back on the mainland, just south of the thriving coastal town of Ayr you will enter **Burns Country**. In this area the beloved national poet of the Scots, Robert Burns, was born, lived most of his very full 37 years and died in 1796. Here are all the echoes of his narrative poem *Tam o' Shanter*, including the Auld Brig o' Doon which has spanned the River Doon in Alloway for 700 years. Burns liked his wee dram and bonny lassies, which seems now to enhance his already monumental reputation in Scotland.

In **Alloway** you can visit the carefully preserved birthplace of Burns: a whitewashed cottage with thatched roof, and a museum devoted to the poet. You'll see the box bed where Burns and three of his brothers used to sleep as children, and such 18th-century implements as a butter churn and a turnip sowing machine. The original of *Auld Lang Syne* is among the mass of Burnsiana in the museum. Even his razor and shaving mirror are displayed.

Nearby at the new Burns Centre, with its accomplished audio-visual presentation, you can decide how much more to follow of the Burns' Heritage Trail, which goes down to Dumfries where he died.

One of Scotland's foremost attractions, **Culzean Castle**, towers above the sea on a rugged stretch of the Ayrshire coast. With it are a country park of over 500 acres (202ha) and stately formal gardens. A Robert Adam masterpiece, the castle dates mostly from the late 18th century and is now a National Trust property. The half-hour guided tour begins in the castle's armoury. The best room is the circular saloon

*A*rran – a beautiful island with a rich past. Standing stones here date from prehistoric times.

75

with its windows overlooking the waves of the Firth of Clyde breaking on the rocks 150ft (46m) below.

Upstairs is an exhibition in honour of Dwight D Eisenhower for his role as Allied Supreme Commander during World War II. In the summer on Sunday afternoons, a pipe

In the heart of Burns Country, the old 'Brig o'Doon' at Alloway hasn't changed for centuries.

band performs on the large sunken lawn of the Fountain Court just below the castle.

Overlooked by many visitors, south-west Scotland has beautiful shorelines, moors and forest scenery, and a castle with one of Rembrandt's great oil paintings. It also claims milder weather than any other area. On the peninsula called the Rhinns of Galloway, the **Logan Botanic Garden** has Scotland's best collection of tree ferns and, among many palms and other warm-weather

species, are superb magnolias from western China.

A nearby natural tidal pool called **Logan Fish Pond** features extraordinarily tame fish that eat from a keeper's hand. At seaside Port Logan (pop. 59) with its little yellow houses, three's a crowd at what is probably the smallest post-office in Great Britain. It measures about 2yds sq ($1.6m^2$). From the most southerly point in Scotland, the high-cliffed Mull of Galloway, the Isle of Man is visible on a clear day.

On a peaceful, pastoral hill midway up the peninsula is a stone chapel which contains several of Scotland's oldest Christian relics: the **Kirkmadrine Stones**, which consist of three stones and various fragments dating back to the 5th century.

South east of Newton Stewart, the small **Creetown Gem Rock Museum** is unusual, if not eccentric. Apart from a celebrated assortment of rocks (including a chunk of the world's oldest feldspar dating back 3.7 billion years from south-west Greenland), you'll

Robert Burns – the 'Heaven-taught ploughman' – is universally hailed the national bard (poet).

also find the largest collection of walking sticks in the world; Gladstone's, Churchill's and Charlie Chaplin's are among those on display.

In the summer, for a small charge, cars (no buses or caravans) can take the scenic 10-mile (16km) **Raiders Road** forest drive from either Clat- **77** teringshaws Dam or Bennan, near Mossdale.

It is well worth making a detour to the north west to visit **Drumlanrig Castle** with its spacious lawns patrolled by sheep on an estate near Thornhill. Of all the treasures in this 17th-century pink sandstone mansion, you'll linger longest over Rembrandt's *Old Woman Reading* on the main stairway, with a fine Holbein nearby. In the drawing-room examine two black ebony inlaid cabinets, which came to Scotland from Louis XIV. Napoleon's dispatch box is also here, a gift from Wellington to the owner of the castle.

South of Dumfries are the lovely red-sandstone ruins of **Sweetheart Abbey**, founded in the 13th century by the Lady of Galloway. It was dedicated to the memory of her husband, John Baliol, whose heart she carried around with her until she died.

On the other side of the River Nith along the coast, the **Ruthwell Cross**, named after its hamlet, is kept in a pretty **78** little church which is surroun-

ded by weathered tombstones. This great monument dating back to the Dark Ages was carved out of brownish-pink stone some 1,300 years ago, stands at 18ft (5.5m) high and is covered with sculpted figures and runic inscriptions. You may have to ask at a cottage along the lane for the key to the church.

Inner Hebrides

SKYE

This best-loved Highland island is outrageously beautiful – whenever *unloved* mists are not swirling around its startling hills and idyllic glens. Fabled Skye is a 5-minute ferry trip from Kyle of Lochalsh, or 30 minutes from Mallaig. Even if you can't stay, Skye is worth a day-trip.

Scenic honours go to two remarkable ranges of peaks: the Cuillins in the south and the Quiraing in the north. They make the island a hiker's or rock climber's idea of paradise. In the rugged **Cuillins** is

Loch Coruisk, reachable by a considerable overland trek or by boat from Elgol. Some say this oblong stretch of blue-black fresh water is the prettiest lake in Britain. Isolated by high hills all around, Coruisk has a beauty which may seem rather eerie.

The **Quiraing** hills are accessed more easily and dominate the landscape just north of the secondary road running between Staffin and Uig, the ferry port for the Outer Hebrides. Go for a peaceful walk among the sheep on the grassy slopes of these dramatic hills.

In the far north at **Kilmuir** are the grave and monument of Skye's romantic heroine, Flora Macdonald, who, disguised as her female servant, smuggled fugitive Bonnie Prince Charlie to safety. It is also in the north that you are most likely to encounter traces of the Gaelic language and culture, now being revived.

On the picturesque coast of Staffin, the **Kilt Rock** is a curiously fluted cliff with a waterfall that plunges down to the sea far below. It is wise to be extremely careful on this lofty green ridge.

Scot, Scottish, Scotch?

Be warned: the Scots do not take kindly to being referred to as Scotch. The following should clear up any confusion between what is Scotch and what is not.

Harking back to that ancient Gaelic tribe (from Ireland), a Scot is a native inhabitant of Scotland. So is a Scotsman or a Scotswoman.

Almost everything which comes from or is typical of Scotland is either Scottish or Scots, as in Scottish hospitality, Scottish romanticism, Scots tongue.

When it comes to whisky, however, it's always Scotch whisky. Also permissible are Scotch egg, Scotch pancake, Scotch mist and Scotch broth.

It all seems perfectly straightforward – especially to a Scot!

79

A mile further on, the Lealt Falls tumble down a long and accessible ravine into the sea at a pretty little cove. Salmon can sometimes be seen leaping here. Closer to Portree you will see a giant rock pinnacle called **Old Man of Storr;** there is a forest walk in the vicinity. Two popular centres for touring are Portree and Broadford, but the island has many quieter places in which to stay overnight.

Dunvegan Castle has been the stronghold of the chiefs of MacLeod for more than seven centuries. On display within this sturdy lochside fortress is the Fairy Flag, a fragile remnant of silk believed to have been woven in Rhodes during the 7th century. They say that it saved the MacLeods in clan battles twice and still has the power to do so one more time. Rather more down-to-earth is a grim dungeon – 16ft (4.8m) deep – into which prisoners were lowered from an upstairs chamber.

From **Dunvegan pier** small boats make frequent half-hour trips to offshore rocks and islets where, if you're quiet, you'll be able to get very close to the seals. There are usually about 20 of them here, but sometimes as many as 200. The seals also appear, less regularly, at spots all around Skye's 1,000 miles (1,609km) of coastline.

In the south the hamlets of Ord and Tarskavaig are worth visiting on a clear day for their splendid views of the Cuillins.

MULL

Peaceful moorland glens in the midst of sombre mountains, unusually appealing shorelines and one of Scotland's prettiest ports are among the attractions of this large western island. From Oban, the regular ferry takes 45 minutes to Craignure on Mull, and there is also a 15-minute ferry link between Fishnish Point and Lochaline across the Sound of Mull. In the summer boat excursions go to several popular smaller islands from Mull.

Tobermory (pop. 700), the island's charming little 'capital', fits snugly in a harbour

*S*heep farming is just one of the industries – both traditional and modern – which have helped to sustain prosperity on Mull.

ringed by forested hills and protected by flat, green Calve Island. Regattas are held here, film-makers use the location, and golfers enjoy a splendid sea-scape from the links just above Tobermory. Somewhere deep beneath the mud at the bottom of the harbour, you'll inevitably hear, is a mass of treasure: in 1588 a gold-laden galleon from the Spanish Armada sank here, but salvage efforts ever since have failed.

Calgary, to the south west, which has probably the best of Mull's sandy beaches, inspired the name of the Canadian city about a century ago.

If you're driving and aren't rushed, take the coastal road bordering **Loch Na Keal**. It's **81**

slow-going but scenic, along a single track beneath lonely cliffs and hills that are mauve with heather. Dozing sheep get up out of your way reluctantly. If you should happen to see an islander – called Muilleachs (pronounced 'Moolucks') – you might hear them talk in Gaelic, which is still spoken on Mull, particularly by the older generation.

At the eastern point, visible from the Oban ferry, stand Mull's two castles, both open to the public. **Duart**, imposing on its promontory, is the home of the chiefs of clan Maclean and dates back to the 13th cen-

tury. **Torosay Castle**, in a sheltered garden, was built in the last century and was often visited by the not-yet-famous Winston Churchill.

IONA

Precious to Scots and revered by Christians much farther afield, this tiny, serene island lies just off the south-western tip of Mull. From Ireland to Iona in 563 came St Columba and about a dozen followers, bringing the Christian religion (and also, quite likely, the Irish secret of how to distil whisky) which would spread through

*W*ith 300 miles (480km) of uncluttered coastline, Mull is an irresistible sailor's paradise.

Scotland. Some 60 Scottish, Irish, French and Norwegian kings are buried on this sacred island. The last was Duncan, murdered by Macbeth in 1040. Centuries of onslaughts by Vikings and others have left no trace of the earliest religious communities.

It takes seven minutes by sometimes bumpy passenger ferry (no cars) to reach Iona from Mull, or there are excursion boats from Oban. The major things to see are: Iona's (mostly) 15th-century abbey, seemingly intact as restored but needing extensive first-aid; a small Norman chapel built probably in 1072 by Queen Margaret; attractive ruins of a 13th century nunnery; St Martin's Cross, carved in the 10th century; and Reilig Odhrain, the graveyard where royalty, Highland chiefs and more recent islanders are buried.

Within the abbey there is an interesting little Benedictine cloister. On a fine day, stroll from here to North End where there are **beaches** of sparkling sand. Most of Iona's inhabitants (less than 100) live in the stone houses by the ferry landing. Sheep, cattle and a few fishing boats indicate occupations, but in the summer most islanders are involved with the throngs of visitors and pilgrims that arrive each year.

Long owned by the ducal Argyll family, this 1,900 acre (769ha) island has since become the property of the government to preserve 'for the nation'. When he visited Iona in the year 1773, Samuel Johnson wrote: 'That man is little to be envied whose patriotism would not gain force upon the plain of Marathon, or whose piety would not grow warmer among the ruins of Iona.'

From Iona you can take a boat trip to nearby **Staffa** island, with its dramatic **Fingal's Cave** which inspired a celebrated Mendelssohn overture. You can also get to Staffa from Mull or Oban.

What to Do

Wherever you might be staying in Scotland, particularly from spring to autumn, there's almost too much to do. Lists of the year's scheduled events fill a thick Scottish Tourist Board booklet, which you can obtain free of charge (see p.126), and you'll come across many other local happenings as you travel around.

Most newsagents in Glasgow and Edinburgh stock *The List* which is a (fortnightly) guide to events, theatre, cinema and clubs in both cities and their surrounding areas.

Special Events

Even if you only want to get away from it all on holiday, make at least one visit to a **Highland Games**, which are staged at various points around the country during the summer months. This can be Scotland at its most enjoyable. Aside from kilted titans tossing a huge pine trunk – the famous caber – and grunting through tug-o'war contests and other athletic endeavours, you'll see pipe and drum bands and Highland dancing, even by quite young children. Members of the royal family often attend the Braemar Highland Gathering, which is held at the start of September. Also of interest are the agricultural shows and sheepdog trials held in a number of farming areas.

Throughout the summer there are country fairs and common riding (when local people ride the 'marches' or boundaries of their town) in the Border region. In July the Scottish Transport Extravaganza at Glamis Castle – exhibition of vintage vehicles, sale of vehicles and competitions – is the largest event of its kind in Scotland. Elsewhere there are excursions to historic castles and gardens, cruises on lochs and firths; kilt-making

Come rain or snow, the Scots are always ready to don a kilt for a (Highland) fling.

CALENDAR OF EVENTS

Apart from Burns Night, most of Scotland's celebrations are local. Don't forget the rugby season early in the year (February/March) and the golf championships in the summer.

January 25   *Burns Night*: Celebrated throughout the country at Burns Suppers: haggis, poetry and bagpipes.

January   *Up-Helly-Aa*: Torchlight procession and an ancient Viking ceremony at Lerwick, Shetland.

March   *Edinburgh Folk Festival*: Bands and music.

April   *Scottish Grand National*: Main event in the Scots equestrian calendar, held at Ayr.

    Kate Kennedy Pageant: Procession of students at St Andrews commemorating the fair Kate, niece of one of the university's founders.

May-August   *Highland/Border Games*: Caber-tossing around the country.

May-October   *Pitlochry Theatre Season*: Drama at the renowned 'Theatre in the Hills'.

May   *Mayfest*: Glasgow's answer to the Edinburgh Festival and Fringe.

June-August   *Common Ridings*: Ceremony of marking local boundaries on horseback in the Borders area.

June   *Royal Highland Show*: Main event in the Scots farming calendar, at Ingliston, near Edinburgh.

August 12   *Shooting season opens*: The 'Glorious Twelfth' and the start of the grouse shooting season.

August   *Edinburgh Festival* : The UK's top arts festival; also the Fringe, Military Tattoo and International Jazz and Film festivals.

    World Pipe Band Championship: World's top pipe bands compete (venue changes annually).

October   *Aberdeen Angus sales*: Autumn show of prime bulls, Perth.

November 30   *St Andrew's Day*: Dinners in St Andrews and around the world.

December 31   *Hogmanay*: Ceilidhs up and down the country.

demonstrations; flower shows; nature walks; geological, botanical and bird-watching expeditions; tours on elderly steam trains; arts and crafts workshops; whisky distillery tours; and dozens of museums, reconstructed mills and crofter cottages. Dunfermline and Edinburgh also have brass-rubbing centres.

Exploring the shoreline, you will spot many different types of shells as well as native marine life; inland, with a little luck you might even find gems and semi-precious stones.

Sports

Without so much as a second glance at castles, museums or the Edinburgh Festival, tens of thousands of holiday-makers arrive in Scotland each year solely to pursue sporting activities. Facilities are excellent for a great range of (more-or-less) warm weather sports, while skiing has become very popular in recent years.

Tour operators, centres and hotels provide package holidays for specific sports as well as multisport programmes for the family.

Golf

Just as Scottish as whisky and probably healthier, golf is a powerful lure for visitors from around the world eager to play the game where it was devised. The surprise is that they can do it so cheaply and easily. If you choose your hotel or a special golfing holiday arrangement with care, you can play a different course each day for a week or a fortnight.

St Andrews, for example, has five courses of its own, plus 12 more within easy reach in north-east Fife. They claim more golf courses per capita here than anywhere on earth. Visitors with ambitions to play the historic Old Course at St Andrews' Royal and Ancient Golf Club, the home of golf, should apply up to six months in advance (depending on the time of year), or enter the daily 'ballot', a lottery to determine which of the lucky applicants will fill vacancies and cancel- **87** lations the following day. Although St Andrews is jammed in summer and everyone wants to try the great Open Championship links, daylight lingers far into the night, so even more people can tee off.

Other outstanding Scottish golf courses include Carnoustie, Royal Troon, Turnberry and of course, Gleneagles.

Fishing

Scotland's rivers, lochs and offshore deeps offer some of the finest **game fishing** to be found in Europe. Much of it is free or very cheap. You don't need a general fishing licence, just a local permit. Casting your line in the more highly prized **salmon** beats, on the other hand, costs hundreds of pounds per week – and you may have to book a year ahead for the privilege.

The Spey, Tay and Tweed are famous for salmon, sea trout and brown trout, though these fish also run in other Scottish waters. Most angling is fly; occasionally spinner or bait is permitted. If you'd like

Links Lineage

How long ago it started in this chilly and windy land isn't clear, but in 1457 James II tried to outlaw golf as a menace to national security: too many Scots marksmen were skipping archery practice and swinging at a little ball instead. That ban didn't work, nor did several others. They say Mary Queen of Scots loved the game so much that she took to the fairways while in mourning for her husband, Darnley. She is thought to have played at Bruntsfield in Edinburgh, probably the oldest course on which golf is still played today. The earliest golf balls were made of leather stuffed with feathers. Not until 1901 was the rubber-cored ball invented. You'll see splendid golf clubs dating back to the 17th century and other historical relics of the sport at the British Golf Museum in St Andrews.

to learn the difference between a dry fly and an insect or how to stay upright while wading and casting in a rushing burn, experts are on hand all over Scotland. Contact the Scottish Tourist Board (see p.126) for publications on fishing around Scotland which give details of the best places, seasons, and necessary permits.

The closed season for trout is from October 7 to March 14, but in some places it's banned for even longer; for salmon rod fishing it runs from some time in October until January or February. Coarse fishing, for perch and pike, is permitted year round and can be very good, particularly in the more southern waters.

Sea-angling trips run from many ports along the Scottish coast and in the islands, or you can fish with good prospects from countless perches on the shoreline. Giant skate

Scotland boasts some of the oldest and best golf courses in the world, often in stunning settings.

and halibut have been caught in the north.

Some species of fish, such as dogfish and mackerel, can be found in considerable abundance, and towards the end of summer you might well hook blue or porbeagle shark.

Scotland's lochs offer popular diversions, from peaceful boating to monster searching.

Boating and Wetter Watersports

You can hire a canoe, a dinghy, a sailing boat, a motor-cruiser or a yacht to explore Scotland's marvellous inland and coastal waters. Sailing schools offer courses for beginners all round Scotland's coast. If you have documentation to prove your proficiency, you may charter larger craft without a skipper; but you can also sail with a skipper and full crew.

On the placid waters of Scotland's lochs you'll be able to waterski – first learning how to if necessary. Some summer days can be surprisingly hot, and swimming is very popular – not all of it in the pools you find at resort towns. Be alert, however, to the possibility of dangerous undertows and rip currents off western coasts.

Windsurfing has become very popular in Scotland and there are plenty of opportunities at all levels either inland on lochs, or on the open sea.

The superb transparency of Scotland's waters make them perfect for scuba diving. There are sub-aqua sites all around the coast, in various inland lochs and on the islands.

For further information on watersports in Scotland write to the Scottish Tourist Board (see p.126) for their free publication entitled *On the Water in Scotland*.

Hill Walking and Mountain Climbing

The most intractable couch potato should succumb to the lure of Scotland's landscape. In the Highlands, particularly, you'll be able to go on nature walks and hill or plateau excursions led by guides who know the terrain well and are trained naturalists. And there are even week-long hikes over moors and glens with food and accommodation included in the package price.

At Glen Coe and Torridon the National Trust for Scotland conducts several superb guided walks which are well worth attempting.

If you 'love to go a-wandering', the open roads and awe-inspiring mountains are ideal for hiking.

Maps and guidebooks can be purchased at information centres near many mountains that are popular with climbers, including the Cuillins on Skye and the peaked ridges of the isle of Arran. A word of warning: despite an energetic safety campaign, large numbers of climbers continue to get into trouble in Scotland. Always get local advice on weather and conditions and plan your **91** route so as to be back before dark. If possible, tell someone where you are going. Above all, never go alone.

Stalking and Shooting

To stalk any of the thousands of Scottish red deer you will need a firearms certificate (obtainable from the area police headquarters), a game licence (from a main post office) and

plenty of money. Some hotels and guest houses have private stalking and shooting rights for their guests on nearby estates at daily rates, justifying the common complaint that deer stalking is a 'rich man's sport'.

The hunting season for red deer stags is from 1 July to 20 October, for grouse from 12 August to 10 December.

Tennis, Bowls, Putting, Curling

A few of the more expensive countryside hotels have tennis courts; Edinburgh has more than 100 public courts. Bowling and putting greens can also be found scattered around the country.

Curling, which you could describe as bowls on ice, is an exciting, fast sport which has been practised in Scotland for at least 400 years.

Try a Scottish safari, arranged by an experienced stalker, if you want to get really close to nature.

Skiing

You'll find instructors, chair-lifts, equipment hire, tows and accommodation at Scotland's three main ski areas: Cairn-gorm, Glenshee and Glen Coe. Snow usually falls from Nov-ember into May.

Pony Trekking and Riding

All over Scotland there are horse and pony centres where you can ride by the hour, half day or full day. Pony treks are normally led by expert guides and may be suitable for young children. Trail riding by horse is only for experienced riders. Some centres offer accommo-dation and weekly program-mes with a different excursion each day. It's a great way to explore the countryside.

Shopping

The ubiquitous sheep are the source of many of Scotland's finest and most famous prod-ucts. However, there are plenty of other locally made items to tempt you.

Shops are generally open 9am-5.30pm Monday to Satur-day (a few places may close Saturday afternoon), and some major stores in the cities also open on Sundays. In the High-lands, however, Sunday obser-vance is the rule. In smaller towns check whether there is an 'early closing' day.

For major purchases many overseas visitors can take ad-vantage of either the personal export or the tax-free shopping schemes. Both systems mean you won't pay VAT (sales tax) on your purchase, but differ in that tax-free shopping allows you to take the item with you on your return journey, but on the personal export scheme the shop undertakes either to ship your purchase to your home address or to have it delivered to your departing flight (see also p.120).

What to Buy

The range of Scottish **woollen products** may seem to be end-less, extending from beautiful **93** designer knitwear, sheepskin rugs and kilts at one end right through to dusters and seat covers at the other. A number of shops specialize in made-to-measure kilts. Harris tweed and cashmere have for many years been best sellers.

There are several major Scottish lines of handmade **crystal**: Edinburgh and Stuart Crystal and Caithness Glass,

Antiques are as popular with Scots as with everyone else, but here they might be a bit cheaper.

which are incised with distinctive thistle or star designs. Scotland also produces some of the finest glass paperweights in the world; leading makes include Selkirk, Caithness and Perthshire.

A great variety of beautiful handcrafted Scottish products are on sale in craft shops all over the country. Look out for the unusual **'heathergems'**, jewellery made from stems of heather, and from Orkney and Shetland the attractive **silvercraft** with designs inspired by Norse mythology. For those with a romantic streak there's

the delicately worked **lucken-booth**, a traditional Scottish love token. Interesting **stoneware** and saltglazed **pottery** from the north and **glassware** from Oban make imaginative gifts. **Heraldic shields** with a crest and a patch of tartan denote your clan. Beautifully designed stainless-steel **spirit flasks** and a marvellous little telescopic whisky tumbler can be ideal partners for that special bottle of malt.

If Scotland has really taken a hold, you may want to go native with a set of **bagpipes**. There are half a dozen suppliers in Edinburgh alone.

Highland oatcakes, fudges from Orkney and elsewhere, shortbread with pure butter, Dundee cake, butterscotch and the incredible array of **Scottish confectionary** may be memorable, if hardly durable souvenirs. Edinburgh rock is a sweet, stick-shaped confection which comes in pink, white, lilac or orange colours.

An obvious choice is **marmalade**, made in this land where it originated: it can be had in a variety of flavourings – whisky, of course, being the most popular.

Scotch whisky is probably no less expensive in Scotland, but you'll find far more brands than you ever thought existed, so take the opportunity to buy an unusual malt while you can.

Children in Scotland

There's no lack of entertaining things for children to see and do in Scotland. Write to the Scottish Tourist Board for its fact sheet on children's activities in Scotland (see p.126). You might also consider some of the following:

In **Edinburgh**, the Museum of Childhood and the Royal Scottish Museum are excellent places to pass a rainy day, and the zoo (in better weather) is always a favourite. **Glasgow** has on offer the Museum of Transport (see p.63 – adults can combine this with a visit to the nearby Art Gallery and Museum) and Haggs Castle, which has a history museum for children.

95

At **Coatbridge**, on the M8 motorway near Glasgow, the Time Capsule puts on all sorts of water and ice amusements, including ice-skating with a woolly mammoth!

Riding and trekking amidst the magnificent yellow fields of rape-seed is the perfect escape.

To see the **animals** of Scotland in their natural settings, visit one of the nature reserves. Three outstanding ones are the Highland Wildlife Park near Aviemore (see p.59), the Loch of the Lowes near Dunkeld (see p.46) and the bird sanctuary of Handa Island (see p.60). Seals and and their pups are the biggest attraction at the excellent Oban Sealife Centre (see p.43).

Pony trekking is a big hit with most youngsters. You can make arrangements for half- as well as full-day excursions in the most popular areas like the Trossachs, Aberfoyle in the Central region, the Borders, around Aviemore and on the islands of Arran (see p.73) and Skye (see p.78).

And whatever you do, don't forget the **Highland Games**, which offer colourful spectacles with plenty of side shows to entertain (see p.84).

For those with very small children, many hotels, guest houses and bed and breakfast premises around the whole of Scotland are well geared up to provide **babysitters**.

Entertainment

The larger cities offer most by way of 'indoor' entertainment, but hotels around the countryside make sure that tourists aren't bored.

Both Edinburgh and Glasgow play host to performances by Scottish Opera, the Scottish National Orchestra and the Scottish ballet, not to mention a wide variety of high-quality theatrical productions all year round. Besides the three-week long **Edinburgh International Festival** held during August and September, cultural high spots include Glasgow's yearly **Mayfest** and the **Aberdeen International Youth Festival**. *Ceilidhs,* or **folk nights,** which are held frequently in all parts of Scotland, feature dancers, pipers, fiddlers and a range of other artists. Folk festivals are staged in centres such as Wick and Inverness. You'll find **theatrical seasons** in St Andrews, Pitlochry, Braemar and Mull, a drama-cinema-music season in Stirling, a Robert Burns festival in Dumfries and a season of Proms in Glasgow.

A wide spectrum of musical styles is covered in **clubs** and **discos**, particularly in the bigger centres, and some remain open until the not so wee hours of the morning (3 or 4am) at weekends.

If you feel like going to a movie, you will find **cinemas** in many towns showing the latest, or at least recent, Hollywood offerings. Alternatively, the excellent Glasgow Film Theatre and Edinburgh Filmhouse offer a good selection of 'arthouse' films. The Filmhouse also provides the focus for the annual International Film Festival held along with the Edinburgh Festival during August and September.

Pubs vary considerably, and while the drinking man's bar still exists, most now have a relaxed and lively atmosphere. Thanks to changes in Scottish licensing laws, children are now welcome in many pubs and families will not be consigned to a draughty children's room. An increasing number of pubs also serve good food, and some now offer live music in the evening.

Eating Out

Not the least of Scotland's many surprises is the amount of good cooking to be found, even in remote spots. Scottish chefs have in recent years won accolades at international culinary competitions. The better hotels and country house hotels may be staffed by award-winning, high-calibre chefs.

Good chefs will make full use of the excellent local basics: fresh salmon and trout, herring, beef, venison, grouse, pheasant, potatoes, raspberries and other fruits. Oatmeal, of course, turns up in all manner of dishes: porridge, oatcakes and oatmeal coatings on such foods as herring and cheese. Samuel Johnson's opinion of oats after he toured the northern regions is still quoted: 'A grain which in England is generally given to horses, but in Scotland supports the people.'

Much Scottish fare is hearty, which helps as a fortification against the weather. Whenever possible try traditional dishes, which are not as exotic as their names sometimes suggest and often delicious. To find hotels and restaurants which serve the best of local produce, consult the *Taste of Scotland Guide*. published annually.

Places and Prices

Although breakfast is provided in abundance by practically every hotel and guest-house in Scotland, restaurants, roadside inns and snack-bars are rather thin on the ground. If you are touring, picnic lunches are a good idea – there is no shortage of lovely sites. For evening meals, most of the finest Scottish restaurants outside cities are in hotels; they usually serve non-residents, but in the summer make sure to book.

Meal times: you may not be served lunch before 12.30 or much after 2pm, or dinner before 7 or after 9pm, in restaurants away from major centres.

Cold? Even in Scotland it can be warm enough to enjoy contintental-style pavement cafés.

In general, restaurant prices compare favourably with those south of the border. This does not prevent certain Scottish establishments, proud of their accolades and perhaps conscious of the shortness of the 'season', from charging prices that would not be out of place in London's West End. The inclusion in the prices of 17½ percent VAT sales tax and, frequently, 10 percent service charge doesn't help either.

Breakfast – and Smoked Fish

The Scottish breakfast, usually included in your overnight rate, is often better than its English counterpart. Oatmeal porridge here is made with salt and served with cream or milk (sugar is frowned upon by traditionalists!) and is a welcome hot starter in summer as well as winter. Apart from fruit juice, fresh fruit, eggs,

sausage, bacon, toast, morning rolls, jams and marmalade, the Scottish kipper and smoked haddock add something very special to breakfast. It is hard to argue with the conventional wisdom that Loch Fyne kippers are best, but it is equally as hard to find a smoked herring from anywhere in Scotland that isn't delicious.

Smoked fish is likely to be appealing to many visitors. The famous Arbroath *smokies* are salted haddock flavoured with hot birch or oak smoke. *Finnan haddock* (or *haddie*) are salted and smoked over peat. Pâtés of kippers, trout, smoked salmon and haddock have become favourite starters in good restaurants.

Soups

Traditional Scottish soups are best if they are homemade. Try the following:

Cock-a-leekie – a seasoned broth made from boiling fowl with leeks and at times onions and prunes. Consumed for at least 400 years and dubbed the national soup of Scotland.

Partan bree – creamed crab (partan) soup.

Scotch broth – a variety of vegetables in a barley-thickened soup with mutton or beef.

Cullen skink – milky broth of Finnan haddock with onions and potatoes.

Lorraine – a creamy chicken soup made with nutmeg, almonds and lemon, and named after Mary of Guise-Lorraine.

Oatmeal – made with onion, leek, carrot and turnip.

Main Courses

Fish and Shellfish: Scottish smoked salmon is famous all over the world thanks to the special flavours that are introduced by the distinctive peat or oak-chip smoking process. Farmed salmon is now widely available, and while the purist may argue that it isn't as good as the wild variety, there are few people who can actually tell the difference.

Thanks also to its readier availability and lower price, salmon is now served in a wider variety of interesting dishes and styles.

The west coast is renowned for the excellence of its lobster, scallops, crayfish, mussels and oysters.

Meat and Game: Scottish **beef** rivals the best in Europe. Whisky goes into some of the sauces served with it: *Gaelic steak*, for instance, is seasoned with garlic and fried in sautéed onions with whisky poured on during the process. Whisky is also used in preparing seafood, poultry and game. *Forfar bridies* are pastry puffs stuffed with minced steak and onions. If you are lucky, you might also find *beef collops* in pickled walnut sauce. Veal is rather rare. In recent years, lamb has appeared more frequently on menus, sometimes in quite ingenious dishes.

Haggis hardly deserves its horrific reputation among the non-Scots. Properly made, it consists of chopped up sheep's innards, oatmeal, onions, beef suet and seasoning, boiled in a sewn-up sheep's stomach bag. Scottish associations round the world serve haggis for their 'Burns Night' celebrations on 25th January. Haggis is traditionally accompanied by *chappit tatties* and *bashed neeps* – mashed potatoes and turnips.

Game still abounds in Scotland, with much of it being exported to Europe. After the opening of the shooting season (the 'glorious 12th' of August) grouse is an expensive, but much-sought-after item on the menu, served roasted or in a pie. It is at its best after being hung for a week or two. Venison frequently appears in restaurants, often roasted or in a casserole. You will also find pheasant, guinea fowl, quail and hare. Terrines and pâtés of game are popular, as are hashes and game pies.

Potatoes are a particular local pride. *Stovies* are sliced potatoes and onions stewed together (sometimes with meat). *Rumbledethumps* are a mix of boiled cabbage and mashed potatoes (sometimes onions or chives and grated cheese are added). You should not have to go all the way to northernmost Caithness for its basic dish of *tatties* (potatoes boiled in their **101**

jackets) and herrings. And in the Orkney Islands they like *clapshot* (potatoes and turnips mashed together and seasoned with fresh black pepper) to accompany their haggis.

Desserts

You'll see various combinations of cheese with red berries or black cherries and vanilla ice cream. *Cranachan*, a tasty Scottish speciality, however differently each chef prepares it, usually consists of toasted oatmeal, cream, whisky or rum nuts and raspberries or other soft fruit. Rhubarb and ginger tart is worth watching out for. Dundee, birthplace of modern bitter-orange marmalade, also contributes a very popular fruit cake and a crumble.

Breads and Dairy Produce

At its best, freshly homemade wholemeal bread is a delicious, crusty, sandy-coloured loaf. Scones, bannocks, pancakes, baps and shortbread are **102** among the great array of Scottish **baked** and **griddled food.** Oatcakes come either rough or smooth, and you'll see them eaten on their own or with butter, pâté, jam or *crowdie*, Scotland's centuries-old version of cottage cheese.

Scotch eggs are deep-fried, hard-boiled eggs coated with sausage meat and eaten hot or cold, often with salad. **Scotch woodcock** generally involves pieces of toast covered with anchovy and scrambled egg.

Scotland produces several excellent cheddar **cheeses**, and recent years have seen a rediscovery of old Scottish cheeses. Produced (although on a small scale) throughout the country, the speciality cheeses are characterized by a high degree of individuality. (If you visit a dairy, cheesemakers will often take the time to explain the process of production.)

Drinks

Graciously, Scotland permits alcoholic drinks other than whisky to be sold within its borders. Because of the country's long-standing association

with France – the 'Auld Alliance' against the English – good **French wines**, especially claret, were brought to Scottish tables before they were widely available in England. Most reputable hotels and restaurants will offer an extensive wine list, which will often include good wines from the 'newer' sources such as New Zealand, Australia, Chile and Bulgaria.

Scotland is proud of its own **beers**. The Scottish equivalent of English 'bitter' is called

Whisky – the Scots' water of life – to the accompaniment of bagpipes. Pure bliss!

heavy, and should be served at room temperature. The 'half and a half' featured in any old-fashioned pub is a halfpint of beer with a dram of whisky as a chaser.

A huge amount of folklore, some say mumbo-jumbo, attends every conceivable aspect **103** of **Scotch whisky**, from its distillation (involving the use of pure mountain water), the aroma of peat and five centuries of expertise all the way to the actual drinking. That there is only one, true Scotch whisky – despite the attempts at imitation – is not in doubt.

The word 'whisky' derives from the Gaelic *uisge beatha*, 'water of life'. It is available in two basic types – **malt** (distilled solely from malted barley) and **grain** (made from malted barley and grain). Most of the Scotch sold today is **blended**, combining malt and grain whiskies. The straight malt whisky is sturdier stuff which comes primarily from the Highlands. It has always been a local favourite and is gaining adherents all over the world. There are now more than 2,000 brands of authentic Scotch whisky.

Purists insist that a single malt whisky should be drunk only neat or with plain water – never with soda, lemonade or ginger ale, which are quite often acceptably mixed with **104** blended Scotch, even by Scots.

After dinner, Scotland's version of Irish coffee, which naturally uses local whisky, may be called a **tartan** or a **Gaelic**. A **rusty nail**, believed for obvious reasons to have associations with a coffin nail, is one measure of malt whisky and one measure of Drambuie. A **Scotch mist** in Scotland is made from whisky, squeezed lemon rind and crushed ice, shaken well. An **Atholl brose** blends oatmeal, heather honey and whisky.

Mineral water is becoming very much part of the Scottish drinking scene. Many Scottish brands are now available.

Coffee and **tea** in Scotland are similar to what is available in England.

Note: Because of a relaxation of the drinking laws in Scotland, you will find certain licensed premises open from 11am to 11pm. Most pubs, many of which now welcome children, are open on Sundays, but off-licences remain closed, as do the alcohol sections in supermarkets. People under the age of 18 are not allowed to drink in licensed premises.

BLUEPRINT
for a
Perfect Trip

An A–Z Summary of Practical Information

A

ACCOMMODATIONS (also see CAMPING on p.108, YOUTH HOSTELS on p.131 and the list of RECOMMENDED HOTELS starting on p.65)

More than 3,300 hotels and 7,000 guest houses and bed and breakfast premises offer holiday accommodation. The Scottish Tourist Board (see p.126) publishes booklets listing many of these establishments, which will have been inspected and graded. There are also many hundreds of self-catering cottages, caravans, chalets, farmhouses, lodges, croft houses (small farms) and flats to let.

Book ahead for Easter, July and August if at all possible. If not, most tourist offices offer 'Local Bed-Booking' services which assure overnight accommodation on the same day. For this reservation you pay a minimal deposit, which is deducted from your bill. Some tourist boards also charge a small booking fee.

Hotels vary greatly in standard. Many of the most pleasant are converted country mansions in isolated settings. Rooms with private bathrooms are by no means the general rule, but some 60 hotels have swimming pools and about 20 have their own golf courses.

In a Scottish hotel, as throughout Britain, you simply sign your name to register. On departure, your bill includes Value Added Tax (VAT) and sometimes a service charge, though this may be left to 'your discretion' (10% is about as discreet as you'll want to be).

The Scottish Tourist Board (STB) lists a great many hotels that have special facilities for disabled visitors and young children and which offer low-season prices for senior citizens.

Guest houses and **Bed and Breakfast (B&B)** premises can be great bargains, although you'll rarely have a private bathroom. Rooms in almost all hotels, guest houses and bed and breakfast places come with hot and cold running water. More and more establishments of all categories are serving an evening meal or high tea.

AIRPORTS

Scotland has four major airports – Glasgow, Edinburgh, Prestwick, and Aberdeen – and some 25 minor airfields scattered about on the mainland and the islands.

Glasgow Airport, at Paisley, handles most of Scotland's transatlantic, European and long-haul intercontinental air traffic. It is a 9-mile (15km), 20-minute taxi or bus ride (buses leave every 20-30 minutes from Buchanan bus station in Glasgow's city centre) and has all the usual facilities required at an international airport – information desk and accommodation service, cafeteria, duty-free shop, and so on.

Edinburgh Airport, which handles European flights and transatlantic charters, is linked with the Waverley Bridge terminal in the centre of Edinburgh, 9 miles (15km) away, by a special bus service that leaves every half hour and takes about 30 minutes. Taxis are available just outside the arrival hall. This busy, modern airport offers a full range of facilities, including car-hire desks, a bank, an information desk, cafeteria, direct-line reservation phones to certain Edinburgh hotels and an accommodation service at the Scottish Tourist Board (see p.126).

Prestwick Airport, about one hour from Glasgow (28 miles/45km), now only handles transatlantic charter flights. The modern terminal, with public bus, train and taxi services to Glasgow and destinations in Ayrshire, has all the usual facilities. Prestwick boasts that it has less fog than any airport in Europe – fewer than 11 hours per year.

Aberdeen Airport, a 7-mile (11km), 35-minute bus or taxi hop from Aberdeen station, serves mainly British and European destinations. It has modern facilities plus a nearby heliport.

Scotland's other airfields are served by **British Airways Express** services.

BICYCLE RENTAL

Information offices at many tourist resorts will direct you to local firms from which you can rent a bicycle by the hour, day or week. The Scottish Tourist Board (see p.126) issues a free pamphlet listing many rental firms. You're advised to book ahead for July or August.

CAMPING

There are more than 600 campsites in Scotland for the growing number of visitors who come here to avoid living within four walls during their holiday. The most elaborate have hot showers, shaver points, flush toilets, laundry facilities, shops and tea rooms, and can offer nature trails, forest walks and even access to golf courses. Many sites are much more limited, with just a handful of pitches. A few of the most attractive locations are operated by the Forestry Commission, which describes them in a free leaflet (see below).

Within Edinburgh's city limits there are three sites, and five others are close enough for easy access. There are also several at Loch Lomond, about 40 minutes' drive from Glasgow. To camp or caravan on private land you need the owner's permission. Without it you may be prosecuted under the Trespass (Scotland) Act, 1865.

Write to your nearest BTA (British Tourist Authority) office for the booklet *Scotland: Caravan and Camping Sites*, or to: Information Branch, Forestry Commission, 231 Corstorphine Road, Edinburgh EH12 6DD, for its listing *Forestry Commission Camping and Caravan Sites*.

CAR RENTAL

As a rule, to rent a car from one of the many local and international firms you must be 21 or more years of age and have held a driving licence for at least 12 months. Valid driving licences from almost all countries are recognized by the British authorities.

CLIMATE

The best months to visit Scotland are May and June, which have the most hours of sunshine and comparatively little rain. The far north enjoys as many as 20 hours of daylight per day in June, and there aren't many of the midges and other stinging insects that become a problem, especially on the west coast, in the full summer. September and early October can be beautiful, but they'll be wetter.

Average monthly **temperatures** in Edinburgh:

	J	F	M	A	M	J	J	A	S	O	N	D
°F	38	38	41	45	50	56	59	58	54	48	42	32
°C	3	3	4	7	10	13	15	14	12	9	6	4

Rainfall:

(inches)	2.8	2.2	2.0	1.7	2.6	2.0	3.2	3.3	2.7	3.3	2.9	2.4

Clothing. Even if you're holidaying in Scotland in mid-summer, take warm clothing and rainwear. Anoraks are very useful: buy a bright, conspicuous colour to warn hunters if you're going to be hiking or climbing. Sturdy shoes are a must.

Scotland makes some of the world's best clothing, and you'll find a very good selection of woollens, tartans and tweeds, although not at significantly lower prices than elsewhere in the United Kingdom.

British and American sizes are compared below, but bear in mind that actual clothing size may vary depending on the manufacturer.

Women's clothing					
Great Britain	10/32	12/34	14/36	16/38	18/40
USA	8/32	10/34	12/36	14/38	16/40
Women's footwear					
Great Britain	3	4	5	6	7
USA	4½	5½	6½	7½	8½
Men's footwear					
Great Britain	6	7	8	9	10
USA	6½	7½	8½	9½	10½

COMMUNICATIONS

Post offices and mail. The United Kingdom offers first- and second-class mail service for letters and packets. Because second-class mail may be slow, it's advisable to pay the modest extra postage and send mail within Britain by first class. Postcards and letters to Europe and other points overseas automatically go airmail.

Stamps are sold at post offices (found in almost every Scottish village even if they share space with grocery shops) and newsagents, as well as from vending machines. You may be given Scottish or English stamps, both valid throughout the United Kingdom.

If you're not sure where you'll be staying, you can receive mail c/o Poste Restante or simply c/o Post Office in the town, free of charge. You'll need a passport or other official identification to pick up mail.

Telegrams. There is no longer a telegram service. Inland telegrams have been replaced by Telemessages, dictated over the telephone, Monday to Saturday, with following day delivery.

Telephones. Public phones are located in pubs, restaurants, post offices and other public buildings, or in phone booths in the street.

British Telecom booths displaying a green band accept only phone cards, which can be bought at newsagents displaying the green sign. Some cabins now also accept credit cards.

Most of the phones in small towns around Scotland and in public buildings are coin-operated phones, which usually take 10p, 20p, 50p and £1 coins. Phones in pubs and bars can work out dearer than phone booths.

Public phone booths display information on overseas dialling codes and the international exchange. To make a 'collect' call, dial 100 and ask the operator to 'reverse the charges'.

The Ski Hotline (tel. 0891 654 654) gives information on skiing conditions in Scotland from October to May.

Faxes. Fax services are available at larger post offices and from businesses offering photocopying, printing, etc. Some airports also now have public fax facilities, similar in appearance to normal phone booths – operating details are given inside the booth.

COMPLAINTS

The local tourist office and/or the Scottish Tourist Board in Edinburgh will want to know of any complaint you have which the owner or manager of the establishment in question has not resolved to your satisfaction. For appropriate matters, contact the police.

In Great Britain consumer protection enjoys legal backing. If an article doesn't correspond to its description, or is defective, you may always return it (provided you've kept the sales receipt). Since the law is on your side, you'll have no trouble from the shop-owner. Proprietors may offer you a voucher for the amount in question, but you have the right to insist on a cash refund.

CRIME

Low by world standards, the crime rate in Scotland is unfortunately rising. Police warn that theft, particularly involving cars and usually invited by carelessness, spoils too many holidays. In hotels, put your most valuable objects in the safe and never leave important possessions in evidence. If you're caravanning, lock up before walking off, and don't leave radios, handbags, etc. near open windows even when you're right there. Do not leave valuables of any kind on view in your car.

CUSTOMS and ENTRY FORMALITIES

For non-British citizens the same formalities apply at Scottish ports of entry as elsewhere in the United Kingdom. Citizens of most Commonwealth countries will require a visa; check with your travel agent before departure. In many other cases travellers need only a valid passport, filling out a short immigration form to enter for a tourist visit.

On arrival at a British port or airport, if you have goods to declare you follow a red channel; with nothing to declare you take the green route, bypassing inspection, although customs officers may call random travellers over to a bench for spot checks. Being caught trying **111** to smuggle anything through the green channel, even an extra carton of cigarettes, is no laughing matter.

As the UK is part of the EU, free exchange of non-duty free goods for personal use is permitted between EU countries and the UK. Duty free items are still subject to restrictions: check before you go.

Restrictions on duty free items obtained outside the EU are: 200 cigarettes **or** 50 cigars **or** 250g tobacco; 2l still table wine **and** 1l spirits **or** 2l fortified wine.

Returning to your own country, restrictions are: **Australia**: 250 cigarettes **or** 250g tobacco; 1l alcohol; **Canada**: 200 cigarettes **and** 50 cigars **and** 400g tobacco; 1.1l spirits **or** wine **or** 8.5l beer; **New Zealand**: 200 cigarettes **or** 50 cigars **or** 250g tobacco; 4.5l wine **or** beer **and** 1.1l spirits; **South Africa**: 400 cigarettes **and** 50 cigars **and** 250g tobacco; 2l wine **and** 1l spirits; **USA**: 200 cigarettes **and** 100 cigars **or** a 'reasonable amount' of tobacco.

Currency restrictions. There's no limit on the amount of pounds or foreign currency you can bring into or take out of Great Britain.

D

DRIVING

To bring a car into Scotland you'll need registration and insurance papers and a driving licence. Seat belts must be worn. Overseas visitors driving their own car will need a Green Card as well.

Driving conditions. An increasing number of foreign motorists are involved in road accidents in Scotland simply because they forget to drive on the left. In the hinterland driving can be a challenge even to British motorists. Many of the twisting secondary roads are single-track, with passing places for giving way to oncoming traffic or for allowing cars behind you to overtake.

When traffic is heavy progress is agonizingly slow as you pull into and out of the side-slips. The form is to wave at the other driver if he pulls off for you. Obviously, you should never park in these essential passing places, even briefly. Other obstacles include sheep and cattle on minor roads, and farm vehicles, which you may encounter on any Scottish road except the limited motorways (expressways) in the central area. Signposting is generally excellent, but you'll need a good map.

Speed limits. In built-up areas, 30 or 40mph (50 or 65kmph); on major roads, 60mph (95kmph); on dual carriageways (divided highways) and motorways (expressways), 70 mph (110kmph).

Parking. There are meters in major centres and vigilant corps of traffic police and wardens to ticket violators, even in small towns. Meters take 20p pieces, ticket machines up to £1.

Fuel and oil. Petrol (gas) is sold by the Imperial gallon (about 10% more voluminous than the US gallon) and by the litre; pumps show both measures. Four-star grade is 97 octane and three-star is 94 octane. Unleaded petrol (gas) is widely available.

Most petrol (gas) stations are self-service. In the more remote areas stations are rather scarce, but you'll appreciate the friendly service when you find one.

Repairs. Most centres have at least one garage for repairs. Members of automobile clubs that are affiliated with the British Automobile Association (AA) or the Royal Automobile Club (RAC) can benefit from speedy, efficient assistance in the event of a breakdown. If this should happen to you, AA members should phone 0800 88 77 66, RAC members 0800 82 82 82.

Drinking and driving. If you plan to drink more than a sip of whisky or half a pint of beer you'd be well advised to leave the car behind. Penalties are severe, involving loss of licence, heavy fines and even prison sentences, and the law is strictly applied.

Road signs. Many standard international picture signs are displayed in Scotland. Usefully, signs announcing your arrival in towns often indicate the number of miles to the next one along the road and from the town you've just left. Here are some written signs that may pose a problem for American visitors:

British	American
Carriageway	Roadway; traffic lane
Clearway	No parking along highway
Diversion	Detour
Dual carriageway	Divided highway
Give way	Yield
Level crossing	Railroad crossing
Motorway	Expressway
No overtaking	No passing
Roadworks	Men working
Roundabout	Traffic circle

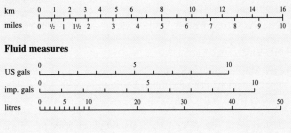

Distance

km   0 1 2 3 4 5 6   8   10   12   14   16

miles 0 ½ 1 1½ 2   3   4   5   6   7   8   9   10

Fluid measures

US gals   0   5   10

imp. gals   0   5   10

litres   0   5   10   20   30   40   50

E

ELECTRIC CURRENT
Throughout Scotland it's 240 volts AC, 50 cycles. Certain appliances may need a converter. Americans will need an adaptor for British sockets, which come in a variety of sizes.

EMBASSIES and CONSULATES
All foreign embassies are located in London, but many countries maintain consulates in Scotland. Check their hours first by phone.

| **Australia**: | 80 Hanover Street, Edinburgh EH2 2HQ, tel. 0131-226 6271 |
| **USA**: | 3 Regent Terrace, Edinburgh EH7 5BN, tel. 0131-556 8315 |

EMERGENCIES

To call the fire brigade, police, ambulance, coast guard, lifeboat or mountain rescue service, dial 999 from any telephone. You need no coin. Tell the emergency operator which service you need. See also CONSULATES above and MEDICAL CARE on p.119.

ETIQUETTE

In shops, restaurants, sports centres, pubs – almost anywhere – local people strike up a conversation once they find out you're a stranger. Scotland (even its cities) is a forthright and friendly place with a long tradition of hospitality. Residents of countryside hamlets, and of the western islands in particular, may overwhelm you with welcome.

G

GAY and LESBIAN

Edinburgh and Glasgow both have a lively gay scene with several gay pubs and nightclubs. The best place to find out details of what's on is the Blue Moon Café, 36 Broughton Street (tel. 0131 556 2788) at the east end of town. The café basement also houses a Lesbian and Gay Community Centre, from which the Edinburgh Gay and Lesbian Switchboard is run (tel. 0131 556 4049). A gay bookshop, the West and Wilde, is at 25a Dundas Street (tel. 0131 556 0079). In Glasgow you can contact the Strathclyde Gay and Lesbgian Switchboard for details of what's on (tel.0141 221 8372).

GUIDES and TOURS

Details of guides and tours can be had from The Secretary, Scottish Tourist Guides Association, 14 East Court, The Thistle Foundation, Edinburgh EH16, tel. 0131 661 7977.

Members of this association wear official badges engraved with their names. Most are based in Edinburgh, Glasgow, Aberdeen and Dundee. Some will travel to accompany tours. A number of transport companies employ their own guides.

LANGUAGE

Just because you speak English, you're certainly not home Scot-free in Scotland. Gaelic and old Scottish words and phrases in everyday use will baffle the most fluent English speaker. Today just over 82,000 Scots speak Gaelic, most of them residents of the Western Isles. 'Proper' English, spoken with a strong Scots accent, can take a while to get used to, and place names are often not pronounced the way you'd expect: Kircudbright is Kir*coo*bree, Culzean is Cul*lane*, Colquhoun is Co*hoon*, Culross is *Coorus*, Menzies is *Mingies*, Dalziell is *Dee*-ell. Here are some examples to help you along:

Scottish/Gaelic	*English*
auld lang syne	days long ago
Auld Reekie	Edinburgh (Old Smoky)
aye	yes
bairn	baby
ben	mountain
bide a wee	wait a bit
biggin	building
bonny/bonnie	pretty
brae	hillside
bramble	blackberry
brig	bridge
burn	stream
cairn	pile of stones
116 ceilidh	song/story gathering

clachan	hamlet
croft	small land-holding
dinna fash yersel'	don't get upset
dram	drink of Scotch
firth	estuary
ghillie	attendant for hunting or fishing
glen	valley
haud yer wheesht	shut up
Hogmanay	New Year's Eve
inver	mouth of river
ken	know
kirk	church
knock	knoll
kyle	strait
lang may yer lum reek	long may your chimney smoke (i.e. may you have a long life)
lassie	girl
linn	waterfall
loch	lake
mickle (as in: **many a mickle maks a muckle**)	small amount (little things add up to big things)
mull	promontory
provost	mayor
sett	tartan pattern
skirl	shriek of bagpipes
strath	river valley
thunderplump	thunderstorm
tolbooth	old courthouse/jail
wee	small
wynd	lane

LAUNDRY and DRY CLEANING

While many hotels accept laundry and dry cleaning, it's cheaper and quicker to take clothes to the laundromats or dry-cleaners you'll find in most Scottish towns. Launderettes often do a 'service wash', meaning you leave your laundry and pick it up within a few hours washed, dried and often folded (but not ironed). This costs a bit extra. Some dry cleaners offer an express service that should take less than half a day. Laundromats and dry cleaners usually close on Sunday (see OPENING HOURS on p.122).

LOST PROPERTY

Whatever you've lost is most likely to turn up at the police station (tel. 311 3131 in Edinburgh, 204 2626 in Glasgow), or enquire at the lost property offices in bus or train terminals.

M

MEDIA

Television. Viewers in Scotland, as in England, have the choice of two BBC television channels (no ads) and two commercial channels. They broadcast in colour from morning – one (Channel 4) until about 2am, the other (Scottish Television) 24 hours. By world standards, output is very good. Additionally, some establishments offer a variety of cable and satellite TV channels.

Radio. There are six different BBC domestic radio stations, including Radio Scotland, which is useful for local news and events. Besides these, two commercial radio stations cover the Glasgow-Edinburgh belt. Various international stations can also be received.

Newspapers and Magazines. In addition to British national newspapers, there are several Scottish daily papers, among which are the *Herald* (published in Glasgow), the *Scotsman* (published in Edinburgh), the *Daily Record* and the *Aberdeen Press and Journal*. Details of events and entertainment in and around Glasgow and

Edinburgh are given in the fortnightly *List*. The *International Herald Tribune*, edited in Paris, and American weekly news magazines are sold in the major centres and at airports.

MEDICAL CARE

Scotland, home of much pioneering work in medicine, is proud of the high standard of its health care. Foreign visitors are entitled to the same free medical care as British subjects, including hospitalization. Private doctors are also available. Edinburgh, Glasgow, Aberdeen and Dundee have major hospitals. Tourist offices and hotels will advise about doctors, dentists and clinics in your area.

Pharmacies. In Edinburgh, Glasgow and a few other major centres you should find a duty chemist (drugstore) open until 9pm; otherwise, contact a police station for help in filling an urgent prescription. If there's a medical emergency, dial 999. Tourist Information Offices can advise you on the duty chemist in your area.

Insects. In the summer midges are a nuisance or worse, especially on Scotland's west coast. Clegs (horse flies) and tiny but devilish berry bugs also attack in warmer weather. Insect repellents aren't always effective. Chemists sell ointments for bites.

Vaccinations. Foreign visitors do not require any vaccinations to enter Scotland.

MONEY MATTERS

Currency. The pound sterling (£) is a decimal monetary unit and is divided into 100 pence (p).
Coins: 1, 2, 5, 10, 20, 50p; £1
Banknotes: £1, 5, 10, 20, 50, 100
   Scotland has its own varieties of banknote, including notes of £1. Spend them during your stay as they may be refused in England (except at banks). English banknotes are legal tender.

Exchange facilities. It's best to change your foreign currency or traveller's cheques into sterling at banks (see OPENING HOURS on **119**

p.122); currency exchange bureaus or hotels rarely offer as good a rate. You can also change money or cheques at some Tourist Information Offices.

Traveller's cheques. All the major types of traveller's cheques are accepted throughout Scotland. You'll need your passport when cashing them. Cheques written against bank cards are cashable in many banks and other Scottish establishments.

Credit cards. Major credit cards may be used in most hotels, restaurants, petrol stations and shops – signs are usually displayed indicating which are accepted.

Value Added Tax (VAT). Almost all merchandise and services are subject to a 17.5% sales tax, or 'VAT'. Foreign visitors can avoid this tax by taking advantage of either tax-free shopping or the personal export scheme.

Purchasers must fulfil certain conditions, and you should note that the schemes are operated only by certain large stores, small, quality stores and specialist shops. If you are eligible, tax-free shopping is the easier option, and your purchase goes with you on the return journey home. If, however, you wish to use the personal export scheme, there are three options: 1) have the purchase shipped directly to your home address; 2) ask the shop to forward items to your port of embarkation (not applicable if you're leaving by air); or 3) you take the goods and a detailed customs form from the store along with you to present at the customs on leaving the country; the tax will be refunded to you in due course.

Visitors from EC countries should present the form to their home customs, who will insert the local VAT rate for the goods. This form should be mailed back to the store where the purchase was made to obtain the refund. Quite a procedure!

PLANNING YOUR BUDGET

Although good value for money is still the general rule in Scotland, bargains are rare and inflation relentlessly does its familiar work.

Accommodations. *Double hotel room* with bath and breakfast, £40-50 per person. *Guest house* (without own bath but including breakfast), £17-18 per person. *Bed & Breakfast* (without bath), £15-16 per person. *Youth hostel* (members only), £3-10, depending on standard of accommodation; breakfast, £2.80.

Airports. *Edinburgh*: bus £3, taxi £12. *Glasgow*: bus £2, taxi £11.

Babysitters. £3.50 per hour (£5 after midnight).

Bicycle rental. £8-10 per day, £40-50 per week.

Buses. Edinburgh to Glasgow, £4 (£5.70 return); Glasgow to Portree (Skye), £14.50 (£19 return). City buses, fares start at 25p.

Camping. £5-6 per tent per night.

Car rental(international company). *Ford Fiesta/Vauxhall Astra* £35 per day (£170 per week). *Vauxhall Cavalier/Peugeot 405* £40 per day (£220 per week). These prices include insurance, VAT and unlimited mileage.

Discos and clubs (Edinburgh). £3-9; average, about £5.

Hairdressers. *Woman's* shampoo and set, £6-8; wet cut, £7-8; cut and blow dry, £10-20; perm, £20-40. *Man's* dry cut, £4; cut and blow-dry, £6-8.

Meals and drinks. Lunch in pub or café, £4-5; restaurant meal with wine, £15-20; pint of beer, £1.60; tot of whisky, £1.20.

Newspapers. British daily papers, 25-50p; Financial Times, 60p; International Herald Tribune, 85p.

Shopping. Pure wool tartan, £15-30 per metre; tweed, £10-70 per metre. Kilt – *man's* £230-300, *woman's* £125-200 (pleated skirt, £25-60). Fair Isle sweaters, £30-40; lambswool sweaters, £25-40.

Sights. Most museums are free. Castles and gardens, £2-4.

Taxis. Basic rate, £1.50 (for 670yds/613m), then £1 every mile.

Trains. 2nd class Saver return: London to Edinburgh, £59 (£69 on Fridays); Edinburgh to Inverness, £33; Glasgow to Wick, £45.50; prices can vary according to day or time of travel – ask for details when buying your ticket. Freedom of Scotland train pass: 7-day, £95; 15-day, £130.

OPENING HOURS

Banks. Open 9.30am-12.30pm, 1.30-3.30pm Monday to Friday. In major centres many banks remain open over lunch and until 4.30-5.30pm. Airport bank/currency exchange offices operate for longer periods. If you need to change money outside these hours, try the local Tourist Information Office as many now operate *bureaux de change*. Some rural points are served only by mobile banks that arrive at regular intervals and stay for a few hours.

Museums, castles, sights. Opening hours vary greatly, but, as a rule, sightseeing attractions are open from about 9.30am until late afternoon or early evening in summer, including weekends. In winter many castles and other places of interest are closed to the public or open for limited periods. Check also for early closing days.

Offices and businesses. Open 9am to 5 or 5.30pm Monday to Friday. Some are open on Saturday morning.

Post offices. Most post offices open from 9am to 5.30pm Monday to Friday, possibly with a noon-time closing outside major centres, and from 9am to 12.30pm on Saturday. Sub-post offices have half-day closing during the week, usually on Wednesday or Thursday.

Pubs. Generally open from 11am to 11pm.

Shops. Open 9am to 6pm Monday to Saturday, with a few closing at 1pm on Saturdays. Large shops and stores (including supermarkets) often operate on Sundays in bigger towns and cities. Bakeries, dairies and newsagents often open before 9am. Many villages and towns have a midweek 'early closing day' when shops close for the afternoon.

Tourist information offices. National and regional centres operate for six or more consecutive months a year, at least from 10am to 6pm Monday to Saturday, and for 4 hours on Sunday. Local centres are open for about 4 months, usually from 10am to 6pm Monday to Friday, and for 4 hours on Saturday and/or Sunday.

PHOTOGRAPHY

You may be forbidden to photograph, at least with flash, certain treasured possessions in Scottish castles, museums and galleries. Well-known brands of film are sold at chemists, souvenir shops, department stores and stationers. Some chemists offer one hour film development.

POLICE

You don't often see any of Scotland's 13,000 regular police, but when you need them you'll find they're extremely helpful. Scottish police are normally unarmed. The emergency telephone number for police aid is **999** all over the country. Police headquarter lines are:

Edinburgh: (0131) 311 3131
Glasgow: (0141) 204 2626

Traffic wardens also function in Scotland and are merciless about ticketing cars for parking violations.

PUBLIC HOLIDAYS

Bank holidays in Scotland tend to be observed only by banks and are not always general closing days for offices and shops (see asterisked entries on chart below for general holidays). Many towns have their own public and commercial holidays, generally on a Monday, when most or all work stops. The Scottish Tourist Board publishes an annual list of local and national holidays, and the chart below is a guide **123** to certain fixed holidays. If one of these falls on a Saturday or Sunday, it is usual to take the following Monday off.

January 1*	New Year's Day
January 2*	Bank Holiday
December 25*	Christmas Day
December 26*	Boxing Day

Moveable dates:

March or April	Good Friday/Easter Monday
May	Spring Bank Holidays
August	Summer Bank Holiday

R

RELIGION

The Church of Scotland, which is Presbyterian, is the principal religious denomination. Roman Catholicism has a strong following in certain areas (100% on some islands). You'll find Episcopalian, Methodist, Baptist and other Christian services. There are synagogues in Glasgow, Edinburgh, Dundee, Aberdeen and Ayr, and a Mosque and Sikh Temple in Edinburgh. Tourist Information Offices can give you details of religious services in the area.

S

SMOKING

If you're a smoker, take full advantage of your tax-free allowance on your journey here (see p.93). The prices of tobacco products in Britain are among the highest in the world, and foreign brands are particularly expensive. Most places do, however, stock a selection of British and foreign brands.

'Thank you for not smoking' has become a sign of the times. You'll see it in indoor tourist attractions like castles and museums and in many hotel restaurants. All buses have seats for non-smokers, and many are now completely non-smoking. Outdoors you're urged to take care with matches, cigarette butts and pipe embers – a great deal of Scotland's landscape is ruinously disfigured by fire each year.

TIME DIFFERENCES

Scotland, like the rest of the United Kingdom, is on Greenwich Mean Time. In summer (between April and October) clocks are put forward one hour.

New York	**Edinburgh**	Jo'burg	Sydney	Auckland
7am	**noon**	1pm	9pm	11pm

TIPPING

Hotels and restaurants may add a service charge to your bill, in which case tipping is not really necessary. Otherwise, menus or bills specify 'Service not included'. You needn't tip in bed and breakfast places. Cinema and theatre ushers do not expect tips.

Hotel porter, per bag	minimum 50p
Hotel maid, per week	£3-4
Waiter	10-15% if not added already to bill
Lavatory attendant	20p
Taxi driver	15%
Tour guide	10%
Hairdresser	10%

TOILETS/RESTROOMS

'Public Conveniences', 'WC' (for 'water closet') or male and female symbols identify toilets in the centre of most Scottish towns, at air, land and sea terminals, in castles, museums, department stores and other public places. A 'superloo' in a big city, for which you pay a small sum, may have showers and shaving points.

TOURIST INFORMATION OFFICES

There is probably no tourist destination in the world which produces more information for visitors than Scotland. Strategically placed throughout the Lowlands, Highlands and islands are some 140 tourist information centres, offering a wide range of publications, free or for sale, as well as expert advice. For a complete list of their addresses, write to the headquarters of the Scottish Tourist Board at the address below. They're identified by blue and white signs with an italicized *i* (for 'information').

In **Edinburgh** take your local enquiries to the Tourist Information Centre at: Waverley Market, Princes Street (tel. 0131-557 1700), or the Information and Accommodation Service at Edinburgh Airport (tel. 0131-333 2167).

The national headquarters of the **Scottish Tourist Board** (STB) is at 23 Ravelston Terrace, Edinburgh EH4 3TP; tel. 0131-332 2433. Don't turn up here for help; only written and telephone enquiries are accepted.

National tourist information can be supplied by any major tourist information centres in Scotland.

The **British Tourist Authority** (BTA) offices in various countries will provide you with information before leaving home:

Australia: 8th Floor, University Centre, Midland House, 210 Clarence Street, Sydney NSW 2000; tel. (2) 267 4666.

Canada: 111 Avenue Road, Suite 450, Toronto, Ontario M5R 3J8; tel. (416) 925-6326.

England: Scottish Tourist Board, 19 Cockspur Street, London SW1Y 5BL; tel. (0171) 930 8661.

USA: John Hancock Center (Suite 1510), 625 North Michigan Avenue, **Chicago**, IL 60611 (personal callers only)

551 5th Avenue, **New York**, NY 10176-0799; tel. 1 800 GO 2 BRITAIN

TRANSPORT

Scotland's extensive public transport network can be of considerable use to tourists. If you're touring the north without a car, a *Travelpass* enables you to ride on most coaches, trains and ferries operating in the Highlands and islands at a significant saving. Maps, schedules and brochures are available at no charge from tourist bureaus and transport terminals. A *BritRail Pass* allows unlimited railway travel throughout Great Britain for 8, 15, 22 days or 1 month, but it must be bought outside Great Britain. Children from 3 to 13 pay half price. The *BritRail Youth Pass* is for young people (16 to 26 years of age).

There are also money-saving excursions, weekend and island-to-island ferry schemes. On the western islands you can take post buses that are scheduled to link up with ferry services.

Various **bus services** cover the metropolitan areas. For Glasgow contact the Travel Centre at St. Enoch Square (tel. 041-226 4826) and for Edinburgh Lothian Region Transport (tel. 031-220 4111). Edinburgh has a good, well-priced local bus service, though it is less reliable at night. Glasgow also has a simple but efficient underground system, which operates in the city centre. Trains are frequent and the standard charge is 50p. The Park and Ride scheme involves parking your car at certain underground stations on the outskirts of the city and then taking the underground into the centre.

Comfortable and rapid **long-distance coaches** with toilets link the major towns. Details from Scottish CityLink, Buchanan Bus Station, Killermont Street, Glasgow (tel. 0141-332 9191).

Train services include the Inter-City trains, with principal routes from London to Glasgow (4½ hours) and to Edinburgh (4½ hours); there are day and night trains. Routes continue on to Perth, Dundee, Aberdeen and Inverness and there are smaller, secondary lines.

For those wanting to put their car on a train from London or other cities, there are motor-rail terminals in Aberdeen, Edinburgh, Perth, Inverness and Stirling.

Ferries. The Isle of Arran ferry departs from Ardrossan, and there are ferry services from Aberdeen to Lerwick and from Scrabster to

Stromness. There are also, of course, many domestic ferries from the mainland to the Western Isles (e.g. Kennacraig to Islay, Oban to Mull, Mallaig and Kyle of Lochalsh to Skye, Ullapool to Stornoway) as well as between the islands. Booking is essential in peak season for the more popular car ferries.

Taxis. In Scotland's major centres you'll find most taxis are the squat London-style carriages where baggage goes next to the driver and you sit behind. They're usually black. A taxi's yellow 'For Hire' sign is lit when it's available. There are taxi ranks at airports and stations. Major centres have 24-hour radio taxi services. There's an extra charge for luggage. You may not always be able to hire a taxi for a long-distance trip (if you do, negotiate the price before setting off). Chauffeur-driven cars are also available (see p.126).

TRAVELLERS WITH DISABILITIES

Disability Scotland publish a directory that covers every aspect of holidaying in Scotland; they also deal with any enquiry on disability except the purely medical. Contact :

Disability Scotland, Princes House, 5 Shandwick Place, Edinburgh EH2 4RG. Tel. 0131 229 2433.

A practical information booklet for visitors with disabilities is also published by the Scottish Tourist Board (see p.126).

TRAVELLING TO SCOTLAND

BY AIR
From North America

Scheduled Flights. Scotland is easily accessible by air from the US and Canada via the three principal cities: Glasgow, Edinburgh and Aberdeen. Glasgow has direct flights from Boston, New York, Chicago, Toronto, Vancouver and Calgary and there are connecting flights from many other Canadian and US cities. During the summer there are scheduled flights between Canada and Edinburgh.

Package Tours and Charter Flights. Various American companies offer a variety of package deals, both for people travelling in groups and for those who wish to travel independently. Tours last from seven to 21 days and often take in English as well as Scottish highlights, though Scotland has now become a holiday destination in its own right. Packages include return flights, travel between holiday destinations and accommodation. Some meals may also be included. Charter flights fly into Glasgow and Prestwick airports.

From England and Republic of Ireland

Scheduled Flights. There are direct services from all parts of the UK to Scotland, including frequent departures from Birmingham, Heathrow, Gatwick, Stansted and Manchester. There are also regular flights from Belfast and Dublin. All routes offer economy fares, PEX, APEX etc. Low-price flights are subject to restrictions such as limited ticket validity, duration of stay at the destination, etc. APEX flights have to be booked at least 14 days in advance.

Package Tours. An amazing array of package holidays is to be had in Scotland, from full board in a comfortable hotel with sightseeing trips to more budget arrangements that may include travel by air or rail to the hotel. Choose between self-catering accommodation, guest houses or a stay in a 'centre' (if holidays with a theme appeal to you). Reasonably priced 'weekend breaks' are another possibility.

BY RAIL

Getting from England to Scotland by train is now quite quick and straightforward, with the trip from London to Glasgow or Edinburgh now taking only 4 to 5 hours. A sleeper service is available from many English towns and cities, and economy fares are offered on some routes.

Tourists can take advantage of a variety of special fare schemes that operate in Scotland. The **Freedom of Scotland Travelpass** is available for either 8 or 15 consecutive days and gives unlimited travel on Scotland's rail network. It can be purchased at ScotRail stations and selected English travel centres. Travelpass holders can also travel on many Caledonian-MacBrayne ferries on the west coast and will obtain a 33% reduction on many Scottish bus routes, as well as on P&O sailings to Orkney and Shetland.

You can also choose from a selection of **Rail Rover** tickets, each one designed to meet the different needs of rail travellers. For the full range of options enquire at British Rail stations.

Visitors from abroad who wish to tour by rail can buy a **BritRail Pass** before leaving their home country. These offer unlimited travel on the rail network throughout Scotland, England and Wales during a consecutive period of 4, 8, 15 or 22 days or one month. There is also the **Flexipass**, which allows journeys to be made on non-consecutive days, for example, 4 days unlimited travel over an 8-day period. These types of ticket *cannot* be purchased within Britain.

If you fancy having your car with you in Scotland but don't relish the long drive up, consider shipping your car on **Motorail** to one of Scotland's Motorail terminals. Not cheap, but a better deal than going by train and hiring a car there.

BY ROAD

Several major thoroughfares (such as the M6 and A1) go up to Scotland, as well as some scenic routes.

BY COACH

There are frequent tour departures from all over Britain to various Scottish destinations, as well as regular coach services by National Express and Scottish CityLink from many parts of the country.

BY SEA

A ferry service links Larne in Northern Ireland to Stranraer.

W

WATER

Rare indeed is the Scot who isn't absolutely convinced that his is the finest and purest water on earth. Its properties are essential in the distilling of that even more treasured 'water of life', whisky.

Bottled **mineral water** is widely available in pubs, restaurants and shops. There's a wide range of good Scottish brands.

WEIGHTS and MEASURES

For fluid and distance measures see DRIVING on p.112.

Temperature

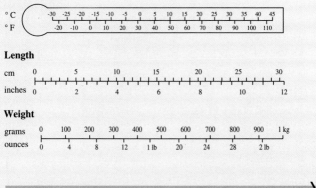

Length

Weight

YOUTH HOSTELS

The Scottish Youth Hostels Association has 80 hostels in Scotland that can be used by anyone aged 5 years or more with a national or international membership card. Facilities and regulations vary. Their address is 7 Glebe Crescent, Stirling FK8 2JA; tel. 01786 451181.

Index

Where an entry is referred to more than once, the main one is in **bold**.

133

135

Other Berlitz titles include:

Africa
Kenya
Morocco
South Africa
Tunisia

Asia, Middle East
Bali and Lombok
China
Egypt
Hong Kong
India
Indonesia
Israel
Japan
Malaysia
Singapore
Sri Lanka
Taiwan
Thailand

Australasia
Australia
New Zealand
Sydney

Austria, Switzerland
Austrian Tyrol
Switzerland
Vienna

Belgium, The Netherlands
Amsterdam
Bruges and Ghent
Brussels

British Isles
Channel Islands
Dublin
Edinburgh
Ireland
London
Scotland

Caribbean, Latin America
Bahamas
Bermuda
Cancún and Cozumel
Caribbean
Cuba
French West Indies

Jamaica
Mexico
Mexico City/Acapulco
Puerto Rico
Rio de Janeiro
Southern Caribbean
Virgin Islands

Central and Eastern Europe
Budapest
Moscow and St Petersburg
Prague

France
Brittany
Châteaux of the Loire
Côte d'Azur
Dordogne
Euro Disney Resort
France
Normandy
Paris
Provence

Germany
Berlin
Munich
Rhine Valley

Greece, Cyprus and Turkey
Athens
Corfu
Crete
Cyprus
Greek Islands
Istanbul
Rhodes
Turkey

Italy and Malta
Florence
Italy
Malta
Milan and the Lakes
Naples
Rome
Sicily
Venice

North America
Alaska Cruise Guide
Boston
California
Canada
Disneyland and the Theme Parks of Southern California
Florida
Hawaii
Los Angeles
New Orleans
New York
San Francisco
USA
Walt Disney World and Orlando
Washington

Portugal
Algarve
Lisbon
Madeira
Portugal

Scandinavia
Copenhagen
Helsinki
Oslo and Bergen
Stockholm
Sweden

Spain
Barcelona
Canary Islands
Costa Blanca
Costa del Sol
Costa Dorada and Tarragona
Ibiza and Formentera
Madrid
Mallorca and Menorca
Spain

IN PREPARATION
Channel Hopper's Wine Guide (will be available in the UK)
Czech Republic